HOT GRAPHICS USA № 2

HOT GRAPHICS USA №·2

Visual Reference Publications

Visual Reference Publications
302 Fifth Avenue
New York, NY 10001

Distributors to the trade in the United States and Canada
Watson-Guptill
770 Broadway
New York, NY 10003

Distributors outside the United States and Canada
HarperCollins International
10 E. 53rd Street
New York, NY 10022

Library of Congress Cataloging in Publication Data:
Hot Graphic USA No. 2

Printed in China
ISBN 1-58471-039-X

Contents

Introduction

Long before writing was created, people replaced written words with pictures. Those who sold goods or services displayed signs above their doors. These were the first visual brandmarks. Today we have more sophisticated ways of relaying the same information. One glance at the pages of *Hot Graphics USA No. 2* will make you realize that photography has replaced the various display techniques used long ago.

Providers of goods and services are increasingly turning to graphic design to create powerful visual tools for establishing and building unique identities that attract and retain customers. It is the ability to escape anonymity and embrace desirable corporate personae that has become virtually mandatory in today's overcrowded marketplace. Graphic design helps market and sell products in many ways, and so too will *Hot Graphics USA No. 2*.

Organizations that wish to position or reposition themselves in the market, define differences between themselves and their competition, signal changes to their clientele, trigger specific intellectual or emotional responses, or attract attention for whatever reason, can turn to graphic design for help.

Graphic design has evolved into a highly condensed form of communication that can deliver its message at the speed of light. The ascendancy of graphic design reflects the spread of international commerce which relies upon visible symbols that are easy to comprehend regardless of language or culture. This visual communication prevails wherever multinational corporations collide in their quest for market share … and *Hot Graphics USA No. 2* showcases some of the best in graphic design.

Alexander Isley Inc.
9 Brookside Place
Redding, CT 06896
Phone (203) 544-9692
Fax (203) 544-7189

580 Broadway, Suite 709
New York, NY 10012
Phone (212) 941-7945
Fax (212) 226-6332

info@alexanderisley.com
www.alexanderisley.com

ALEXANDER ISLEY INC.

Alexander Isley Inc. was founded in 1988 to do work that communicates with intelligence, sensibility, and a point of view. Over the years, our experienced team of designers has earned the trust of a diverse range of clients while establishing an international reputation for innovative, influential, and effective work.

Our expertise lies in the design and development of promotional materials, corporate communications, and publications. Alexander Isley Inc. is also well known for award-winning work in the areas of architectural signage, retail merchandising, packaging, and exhibition graphics.

With offices in New York and Connecticut, we provide all services relating to research and design while overseeing all aspects of implementation. We form design and support teams for each of our clients in order to provide attentive collaboration and service over the course of every assignment.

We come from different design, marketing, and technical backgrounds. In addition to the staff design group, Alexander Isley Inc. has in-house account and project management support. In order to provide full service to our clients, we often work with our affiliated marketing company, The Dave and Alex Show, a full-service advertising and marketing communications firm. The combined capabilities of our companies enable us to provide comprehensive brand positioning, marketing, and design services.

We attribute the success of our company's work to our history of collaborating with clients who have a strong belief in the value of their own products and services. We begin each assignment by thinking about what a design should do rather than focusing on what it should look like. More than anything else, however, what sets Alexander Isley Inc. apart is the stubbornly unusual way in which we approach our assignments: We assume that our audiences are smart.

Our work is represented in the permanent collections of the Cooper-Hewitt Museum, the Smithsonian Institution's National Design Museum, the San Francisco Museum of Modern Art, and the YCS Design Library in Japan. Our projects have been exhibited at the Georges Pompidou Center and the New York Art Directors' Club and have been featured in *Time*, *Communication Arts*, *I.D.*, *Print*, *Entertainment Weekly*, *Metropolis*, *Blueprint*, and *Architectural Record*.

Prior to establishing the firm, Alexander Isley was senior designer at Tibor Kalman's influential M&Co. and art director of the fearless, much-missed, and much-imitated *Spy* magazine.

I'M A CUSTOMER.

WHO ARE
YOU?

MOVE ME

WE'RE GOING TO DO IT **MY** WAY

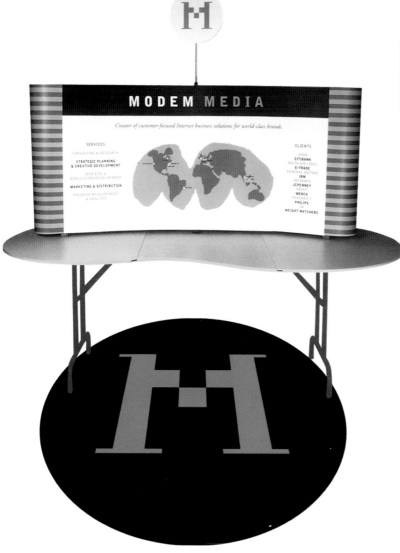

MODEM MEDIA

Creator of customer-focused Internet business solutions for world-class brands.

Above:

Modem Media
Norwalk, CT

Development of a positioning and capabilities book for a premier Internet marketing firm. Unlike an ordinary corporate communications piece, this book presents an engaging narrative that pulls the reader through and positions our client as knowing its audience. The project included designing, writing, and commissioning all photography. It was produced by The Dave and Alex Show.

Below:

Modem Media
Norwalk, CT

Creation of a series of portable job-fair booths. Most of these types of things are a banner on a pole; we made this a bit more elaborate— but it still breaks down to fit into a case for easy portability.

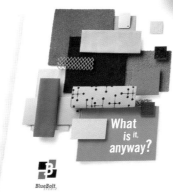

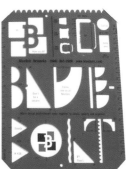

BlueBolt Networks
Durham, NC

Development of a comprehensive identity and marketing communications program for a company providing specification products and services to the architectural and interiors communities. Alexander Isley Inc.'s responsibilities included the development of a brand personality and marketing platform, product naming, graphic identity, sales materials, interface design, trade show booths, education program, and advertising.

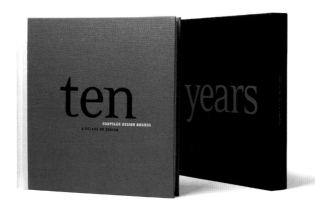

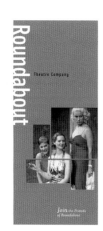

Daimler Chrysler

Detroit, MI

Design of a book commemorating 10 years of winners of the prestigious Chrysler design awards. The design includes an unusual cover and slipcase, making it as much an object as it is a book.

Left:

Roundabout Theatre Company

New York, NY

Development of identity and communications materials for a landmark New York City cultural institution.

1

2

3

4

5

6

7

8

9

10

11

12

13

14

15

16

17

18

19

20

1 Architectural firm
2 Designer Alexander Julian
3 Moby-Dick Wharf Restaurant
4 Shoe retail chain
5 Fashion brand
6 Still-life photographer
7 Online community
8 Concert series
9 Home-building consultant
10 Chain of music stores
11 Retail chain
12 Restaurant
13 Museum exhibition
14 Film festival
15 Toy marketing company
16 Children's arts program
17 Film title for Nickelodeon
18 Home furnishings designer
19 Museum exhibition
20 Museum identity

Discovery Channel School

Silver Spring, MD

Development of a packaging program and style guide for Discovery Channel School, the educational/in-school division of Discovery Communications. Our responsibilities included designing product packaging systems for the educational market as well as writing and designing the style guide for licensee use. The cover is a white marker board that can be tailored to the recipient.

JobDirect/Korn Ferry

Stamford, CT

Development of an overall marketing and communications program for an online recruiting service focusing on the entry-level marketplace. Part of the campaign included design of a trade show environment based on our positioning that "We see it differently." We ran a series of upside-down teaser ads and followed them with this purposely cheesy upside-down trade show booth. Created by The Dave and Alex Show.

MalCONTENT Conference

New York, NY, and San Francisco, CA

Development of an identity, positioning, and conference materials for the inaugural MalCONTENT conference. The general theme of the event centered around the notion that, way back in 2000, the Internet world was riding high and that people should beware. (How prescient.) Created by The Dave and Alex Show.

15

Reebok

MasterCard

AOL Time Warner

Memorial Sloan-Kettering Cancer Center

Hearst Corporation

Accenture

Creative Touch Interiors

Texaco

Van kampen Funds

Corporate Communications

Through the development of corporate literature, capabilities kits, view books, media kits, annual reports, and recruitment brochures, Alexander Isley Inc. understands the intricacies and challenges inherent in each corporate communications assignment. We dedicate ourselves to the mission of embracing a unique and appropriate strategy. Through careful study, thorough strategic planning, smart writing, and memorable design, we bring out each client's unique visual voice.

Selected Clients

Accenture
American Lung Association
American Museum of the Moving Image
Animal Planet
AOL Time Warner
Brooklyn Academy of Music
Canon USA
City of New York
Cooper-Hewitt National Design Museum
CSFBdirect
Daimler Chrysler
Discovery Communications Inc.
Forbes FYI
Giorgio Armani
Hearst Corporation
iVillage
JobDirect/Korn Ferry
Jonathan Adler
Lend Lease
Liberty Science Center
Linens N Things
Lowe's
MasterCard

Memorial Sloan-Kettering Cancer Center
Modem Media
MTV Networks
National Endowment for the Arts
New York Women in Communications
Nickelodeon
Polaroid
Polo/Ralph Lauren
Random House
Reebok International Ltd.
Revlon
Rock and Roll Hall of Fame and Museum
Roundabout Theatre Company
Scholastic
ScreamingMedia
Sony Wonder
Sports Illustrated
Texaco
Time
Timex Corporation
Toys "R" Us
Van Kampen Funds
WHSmith Ltd.

ALLEMANN ALMQUIST & JONES

We have a simple philosophy: *connect with clarity*. As one of the East Coast's leading design firms, we have adhered to this principle for more than 15 years. We work both in print and on the Web; marketing and corporate communications; corporate identity and branding. Our clients include a broad range of large companies, start-ups and prominent not-for-profit organizations.

What unites them all is the desire to connect with their audiences through communications design that accurately reflects the personality and culture of their organizations. We help clients to rise above the clamor by enabling them to communicate in their organization's true voice.

Allemann Almquist & Jones
124 North 3rd Street
2nd Floor
Philadelphia, PA 19106

T: 215.829.9442
F: 215.829.1755

www.aajdesign.com

ESTABLISH A BRAND

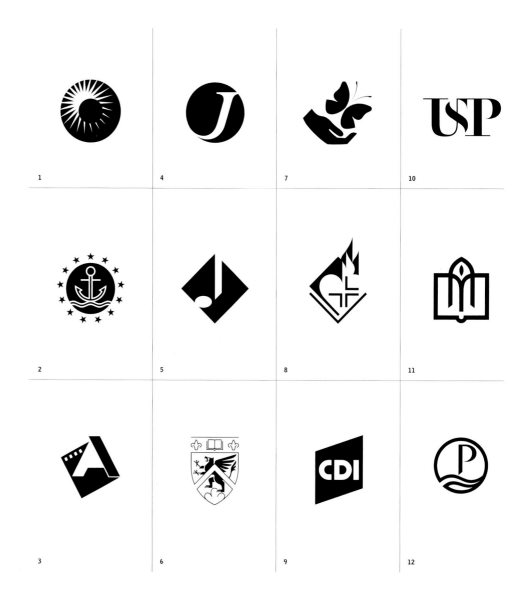

1 Franklin Institute
Science Museum

2 Independence
Seaport Museum

3 Abbey Camera

4 Jefferson Health
System

5 Delaware Symphony
Foundation

6 Chestnut Hill College

7 Children's
Rehabilitation
Hospital

8 Order of
Saint Augustine

9 CDI Corp.,
Technical Staffing
and Outsourcing

10 University of
the Sciences in
Philadelphia

11 DeSales University

12 Portside, Waterfront
Condominiums

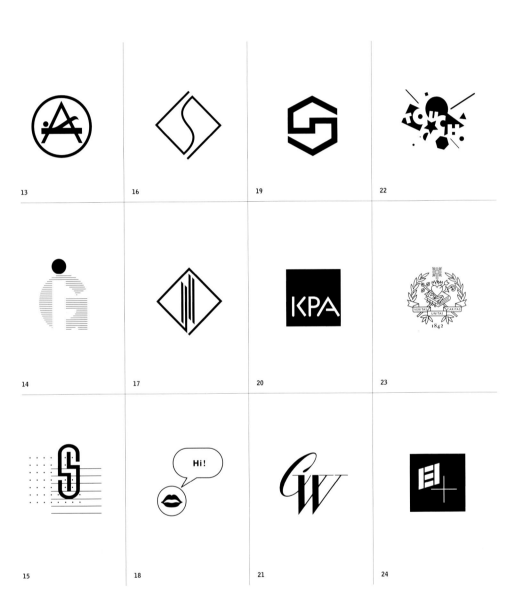

13

16

19

22

14

17

20

23

15

18

21

24

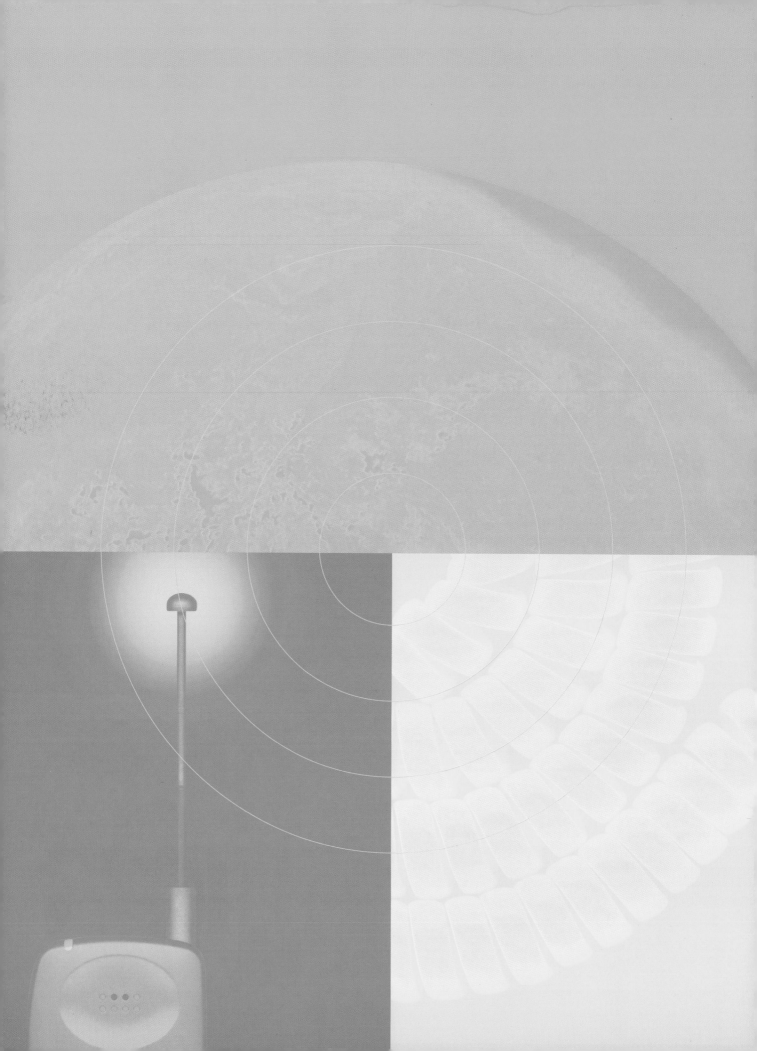

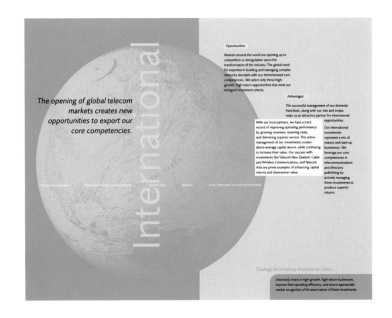

25

26

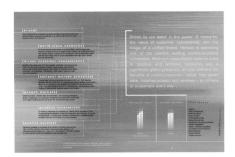

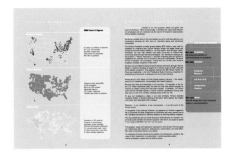

26

25 Bell Atlantic and Nynex Merger Brochure
26 Bell Atlantic Investor's Reference Guide, 1997
27 Verizon Annual Report, 2001

28

29   **30**

31

32

 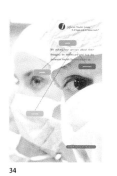 

33   **34**   **35**

First Two Rows
The Franklin Institute Science Museum
28 Logo
29 News & Events
30 Future Center Brochure
31 Upcoming Exhibition Poster Series

Third Row
Jefferson Health System
32 Logo
33 Annual Report 2000
34 Annual Report 2001
35 Identity System Signage Application

48

49

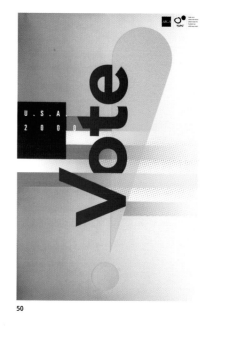

50

48 The University of the Arts
Graphic Design Department
Lecture Series Poster

49 Philadelphia Center City
District Poster

50 AIGA Election Poster

Antista Fairclough
Design for Brand Building
64 Lenox Pointe N.E.
Atlanta, Georgia 30324
404-816-3201

A N T I S T A   F A I R C L O U G H

Design for Brand Building

Retail Store Design · Quick Service Restaurant Design

Petroleum Station & Convenience Store Design

Corporate Identity · Brand Identity · Industrial Design

Packaging, Labeling & Strategic Brand Analysis

and imagery
if impact
& strategy

1- Viva Towels brand revitalization, identity and
packaging design.

2- King Cobra brand revitalization, primary and
secondary packaging design.

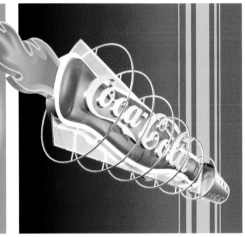
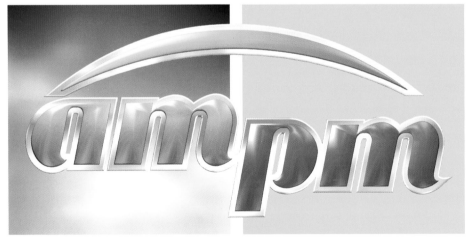
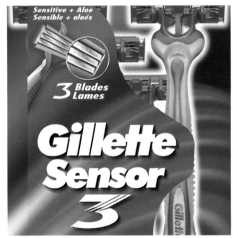

FASHION EYEWEAR

1- Lipton ChiaLatta new product identity and packaging system development.

AXIOM CREATIVE GROUP

Axiom Creative Group
1445 S. Mint Street
Charlotte, North Carolina 28203
704.376.3003
www.axiomcg.com

Lots of people say lots of things about branding, design and the power of visual communications. Most of it is sheer nonsense. But there are a few things, core principles, that are worth believing in. These few principles are so fundamental to doing smart work that you might call them axioms. But when we work with our clients we don't really talk about these principles. We just demonstrate them.

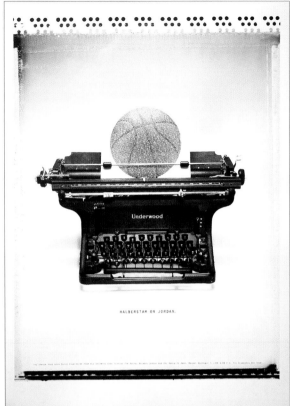

1   2

1. Announcement poster for a reading at the Algonquin in New York for David Halberstam's new biography on Michael Jordan. Actual excerpts from the book make up the image of a basketball.

2. Educational Series Poster for a Sappi Paper workshop to illustrate the basics of the printing process.

3. Brochure celebrating World T.E.A.M. Sports' five years of raising awareness and uniting the diverse capabilities of all people through sports.

4. Little and Associates Architects Annual Report highlighting their community involvement.

5. A direct mail piece for the *Fortunate Few* program, a select group of corporate sponsors and individuals who have made substantial contributions to World T.E.A.M. Sports.

6. Direct mail for Transamerica's *Extra Variable Annuity Fund*, sent to brokers and their managers.

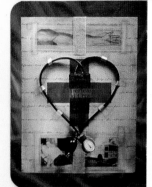

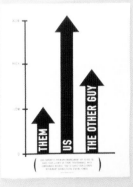

Profero Identity Systems

Formily known as Interfic USA, Profero needed a new brand identity system to better represent their revolutionary corrugated fiberboard designs and production processes.

Our solution was to break the new identity down into it's basic elements: *pinpoint solutions* (triangle); *solid service* (square); and *complete product solutions* (circle). This four-part series began with a general announcement and was followed up with a series of mailings that explained Profero's core values. We used bright colors, simple layouts, existing photography and even embossed cardboard mailers to cut through the mail clutter that the target audience of engineers constantly receives.

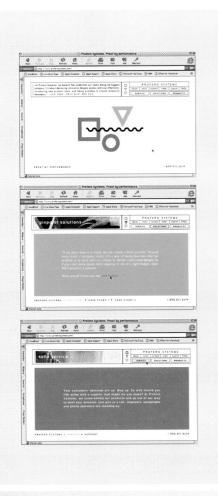

First Trust Bank Direct Mail Series

First Trust Bank's considers the small business account holder their specialty and wanted to grow this business. Recognizing that most prospects already do their banking with larger banks, the frustrations with; lack of personal contact, few or no callbacks, and hassles with obtaining loans, seemed like fertile ground. Especially because First Trust is more responsive and easier to deal with than larger banks. (So much so, they often know their clients by name).

We developed the "Traditional Bank Tool Kit", filled with items a small business owner might find helpful when dealing with a large bank. The tools included; a magic 8 ball to answer banking questions when no one's feeling helpful, a signal mirror to contact their banker when they can't get someone on the phone calls, and finally a crowbar to help them pry a loan check away from their banker. Each piece included an instruction book on how to use the tool and was summed up by pointing out that people who bank with First Trust don't need any of these tools, because they don't have any of these problems.

no show.

mohawk options
winter white
80 cover

1

2-4

1. A paper promotion commissioned by Mohawk promoting the high opacity and other benefits of their Options line of papers to an audience of designers and printers.

Our solution was to create the fictional character of 'Moe Hawke'. This frustrated paper technician becomes so fed up by the fact that no one understands how well Options paper prevents 'show-through' that he strikes out on his own. Along the way he shows that not only can Options solve printing problems, but it's wonderful opacity can also help block out unpleasant things in life.

2. Internet Soccer :30 second video identity used for presentations to international soccer organizations like FIFA as well as plain ol' rabid soccer fans.

3. Mike Carroll Photography website.

4. Wachovia Securites Benefit Services Group DVD promoting the advantages of enrolling in a retirement plan.

The Hopewell Titans, a high school identity

Guinness Gurus, a local co-ed softball team

BigSea, an internet solutions provider

TeamUp, a non-profit sports organization that develops programs for inner-city youth

Face of America 2002, a cycling event from Ground Zero to the Pentagon

Face of America 2001, a sporting event promoting health, fitness and the environment

Weenie Roast, a logo for an all-day outdoor concert sponsored by 106.5 fm

Pet Au Pair, a young, upscale petsitter

Workers Unite, t-shirt graphic for an employee community event with Habit for Humanity

David Neff Photography, an identity for a local photographer

Titans, secondary logo and mascot

All Sports Day, an event where professional athletes give one-on-one instruction to inner city youth

The Fire, an identity for a local indoor youth soccer team

Southend Beverage, a local beer, wine and liquor store logo

Fury, an FMC pesticide protection product for soybean farmers

Royale Resorts, an upscale retirement community

Team Angry Monkey, t-shirt graphic for an employee bowling tournament

The Fly, a rollercoaster ride owned by Paramount Parks

Internet Soccer, an internet resource for soccer enthusiasts

Gauntlet, an FMC agricultural protectant for farmers

1743 Wazee St.
Suite 321
Denver, CO 80202
t 303.296.1133
f 303.296.1192
www.beauchampgroup.com

energized | creativity

beauchamp) g r o u p

Anticipation. This was the emotion that we created through a hologram designed to announce the debut of the Guggenheim Museum in Bilbao, Spain. It was a unique opportunity to connect the museum with a compelling Brand experience and to spark expectation of a tactile experience and the "take away memories" that follow immersion in an exhibition environment.

We created these experiences with the curb appeal at the CityCenter Englewood mixed-use development and at the Farnborough Air Show Exhibition in the UK. The story we delivered in print educated visitors at Farnborough about the manufacture of an exotic metal that improves your golf game with a higher launch and more range and adds endurance to a long distance mountain bike trek.

Our creative story begins in historic loft offices in lower Downtown Denver (LODO). We begin each project with a commitment to "Energized Creativity", our name for bringing a strong sense of purpose to the job of crafting a spirited brand experience.

We collaborate with great creative resources and clients worldwide to develop tradeshow exhibits in Monte Carlo, San Francisco, Las Vegas, Orlando, and New York. We also produce two-dimensional projects for clients in Denver, Milan, Paris, and Birmingham, England, connecting our clients' brands with the world and building more persuasive brand images that speak to more people everywhere.

1 CityCenter Englewood Wayfinding Signage and Community Kiosk

e n v i r o n m e n t a

2 ForestCity Stapleton Visitor Center Identification and Wayfinding

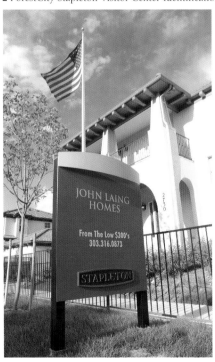

r a p h i c s

3 Gallery Place Themed Signage

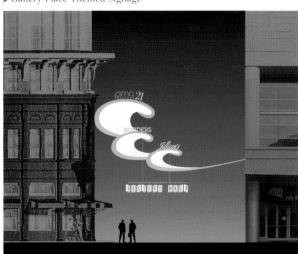

4 Chambers Office Centre Identification Signage

5 Cub Square Retail Graphics

1 TIMET Exhibit / ITA San Francisco

2 TIMET Exhibit / ITA Las Vegas

3 TIMET Product Displays / ITA San Francis

4 TIMET Exhibit / ITA Las Vegas

5 TIMET Exhibit / ITA Las Vegas

6 Arvin/General Motors
Interactive Muffler Exhibit

e x h i b i t i o n s

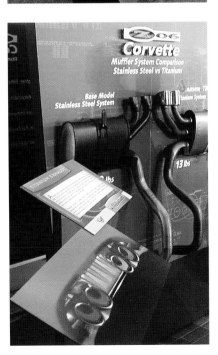

1 TMG Marketing Brochure

print collateral

2 Tremont 2001 Annual Report

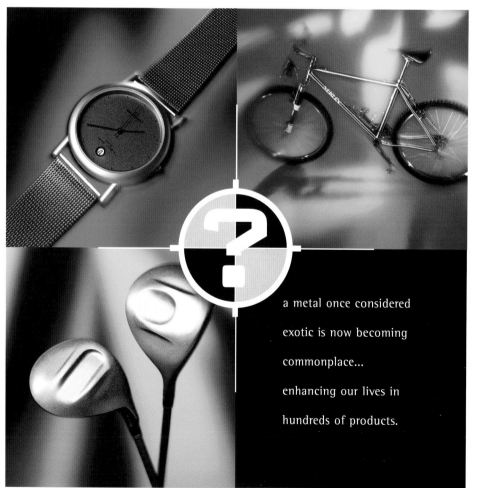

a metal once considered
exotic is now becoming
commonplace...
enhancing our lives in
hundreds of products.

3 TIMET Consumer Brochure

1 Tribekka ID and Shopping Bag

2 NonPareils ID and Shopping Bag

3

4

5 Summerfest Evergreen

6 Celebrate Colorado Artists

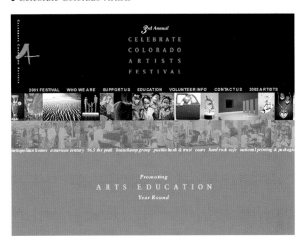

corporate ID & new media

7 TIMET Website

47

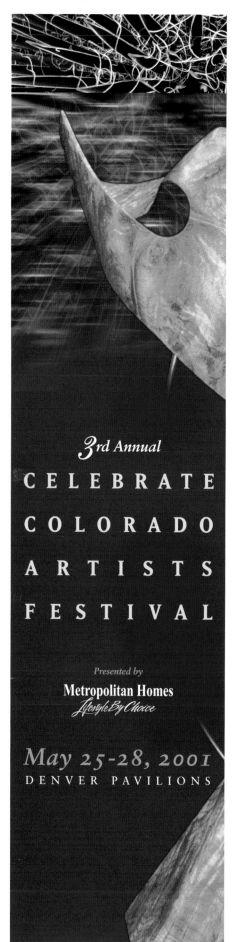

integrated branding

Celebrate Colorado Artists Festival Promotional Campaign. The campaign included 60' tall banners, 40' tall blade signs, a 80'x30' slide presentation presented on the downtown Denver Pavilion's exterior wall, elevator graphics, Artist's application, postcards, program and many other mediums to increase community awareness. Beauchamp Group began the process of developing CCOA's image when they first came to life. Attendance grew 600% in the four years we worked with the organization, and has become one of the most highly recognized arts festivals in the country.

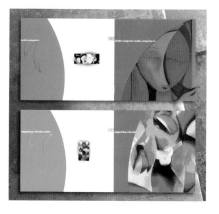

Brainstorm
9820 Westpoint Drive
Suite 400
Indianapolis, Indiana 46256
317.558.1800
toll-free 1.866.558.1870
info@getzapped.com
www.getzapped.com

BRAINSTORM

At Brainstorm, our course is guided by a unique passion for excellence in benefit-driven solutions. Our positioning statement, "because we think harder," speaks to the fact that we think strategically on behalf of our clients in solving their communication challenges and enhancing their marketing opportunities. Our goal is to help each client to accomplish outlined objectives. Whether those goals include increasing revenues, advancing efficiencies, lowering expenses or fostering new and repeat business, we always look to positively affect the quality of our clients products and services. Through our proprietary, strategic, market-driven process, called THINK benefit™, we provide tangible, quantifiable results that give our clients the competitive edge. That's why *U.S. News & World Report* called Brainstorm: "a new breed of consultant."

Brainstorm offers a complete approach to marketing needs that is rooted in analysis as well as creativity. Before we begin a project, we first consider what the finished product should accomplish, not simply what graphic elements it should contain. From conception to completion, our integrated, strategic design services include corporate, brand and product identity; print collateral; multimedia presentations; web development; consumer packaging and sales collateral materials including business-to-business as well as business-to-consumer based initiatives.

Our vision is to be a creative partner for our clients, to deliver innovative and effective solutions that meet every marketing challenge and to expand organizations to encompass new and limitless opportunities.

FUSING brand strategy and proven business solutions with integrated web, print, multimedia and concept development

1

1. Indy 500 Brand Identity
2. Motorola Interactive

2

1

2

3

1. CMK Collateral
2. Thomson Interactive
3. SpotCast Collateral
4. RCA Dome Brand Identity
5. 2Die4 Collateral

4

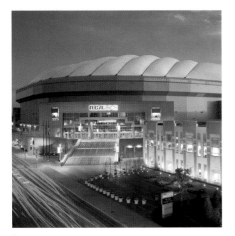

5

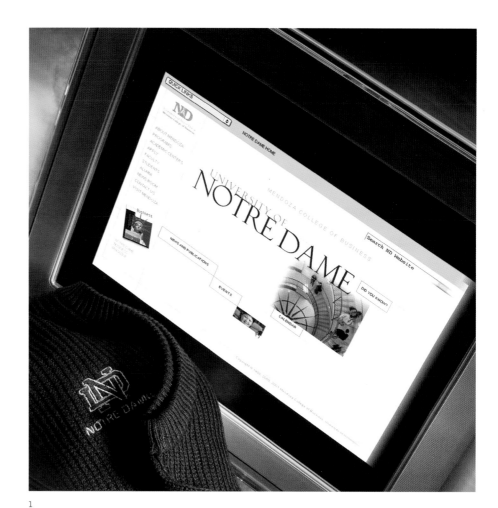

1

1. University of Notre Dame Web Initiative
2. RCA Scenium Collateral

2

1

2

3

the enigma™

4

FORMULA 1
INDIANAPOLIS
UNITED STATES GRAND PRIX

5

RCADOME

6

1. RCA Collateral
2. Study Abroad Foundation Brand Identity
3. Bottled Software Brand Identity
4. Fanimation Brand Identity
5. F1 U.S. Grand Prix Brand Identity
6. RCA Dome Brand Identity

1

1. Ernest Hemingway Catalogue/Brand Identity
2. CMK Collateral
3. RCA Retail Display

2

3

BRAINSTORM

1

2

3

4

1. Harper Direct Mail
2. I-Teams Give & Go Web Initiative
3. EMI Records Web Initiative
4. Indy 200 Brand Identity
5. Brickyard 400 Brand Identity
6. GE/RCA/Thomson Web Initiative

5

6

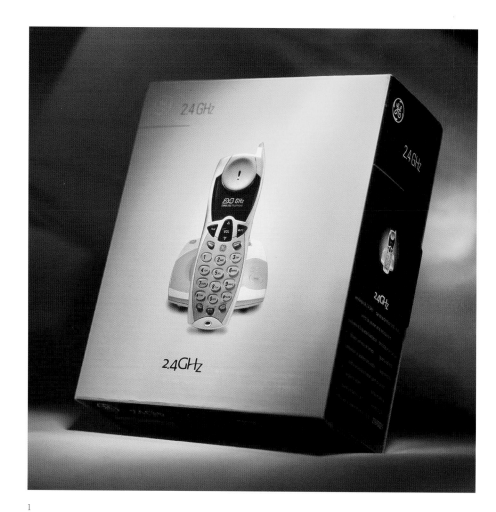

1. GE Consumer Packaging
2. EBSCO Retail Brand Identity
3. Motorola Brand Identity
4. Cry International Foundation Brand Identity
5. ATOM Records Brand Identity

1

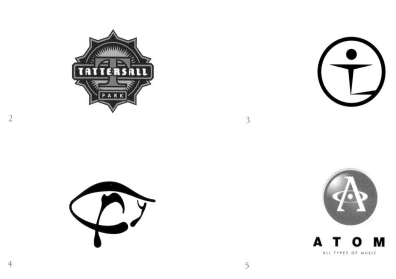

2

3

4

5

Cahan & Associates
171 Second Street, Fifth Floor
San Francisco, CA 94105
415.621.0915
www.cahanassociates.com

CAHAN & ASSOCIATES

Cahan & Associates possesses a unique ability for honing in on a singular, emotional truth that makes people care. While the San Francisco-based design agency is widely praised for its evocative annual reports, it has also gained significant recognition for its product packaging, brand identity, direct mail, advertising and web design. Whatever the creative challenge, the goal is the same: to peel away the marketing and expose the kernel of truth within.

To do so, the agency's founder and creative director, Bill Cahan, leads his designers on an intellectual journey into a client's business and challenges. Cahan's passion for fresh thinking is reflected in his team's commitment to doing hours and hours of research before a single design layout is attempted. It's the kind of in-depth analysis that clients often wish they had the time to do themselves—and it uncovers creative paths that are unique, original and quite often groundbreaking.

"Our range of solutions is varied because it reflects our client's message and culture, not our own," says Cahan, which helps explain not only the diversity of creative thinking at Cahan but also the diversity of clients.

From Fortune 500 companies to emerging growth companies, from high tech and biotech leaders to sporting goods and dry goods makers—Cahan thrives on finding new problems to be solved. This is in large part because the agency's founder is so easily bored with repeating ideas and approaches.

That "impatience," as Cahan himself calls it, has fueled the agency's success for more than 18 years, a track record that includes winning over 2,000 awards, segments on CNN and CNBC, and write-ups in hundreds of periodicals and books. Cahan's penchant for refreshing the stodgy world of annual reports is being chronicled in *Cahan & Associates on Annual Reports*, in bookstores Spring 2004. And Princeton Architectural Press has released a book on Cahan & Associates titled "I Am Almost Always Hungry," which is highly regarded among design professionals nationally and internationally.

By any measure, one word best sums up the work of Cahan & Associates: Smart. Time and again, Cahan and his staff have demonstrated that design driven by thoughtfulness is design that ends up being memorable.

1

Monday, September 24

1. AIGA VOICE Brochure.
   Creative director: Bill Cahan.
   Art directors: Bill Cahan, Michael Braley,
   Kevin Roberson, Bob Dinetz, Sharrie Brooks.
   Designers: Michael Braley, Bob Dinetz,
   Sharrie Brooks, Kevin Roberson, Gary Williams.
   Photographers: Kevin Roberson, Bob Dinetz,
   Sharrie Brooks. Illustrators: Gary Williams,
   Bob Dinetz. Copywriters: AIGA, Bob Dinetz,
   Kevin Roberson, Gary Williams.

EFFEN™

VODKA

IMPORTED
FROM
HOLLAND

750ML | 40% ALC. BY VOL. | (80 PROOF)

2

2. jstar Brands Effen Vodka.
Creative director: Bill Cahan.
Art directors: Bill Cahan, Michael Braley.
Designers: Michael Braley,
Todd Simmons.

While companies look for ways to cut
expenditures in response to economic downturn,
the majority of our client relationships remain intact.
In most cases, they strengthen.

TO OUR SHAREHOLDERS: Gartner had a good year in difficult times, and we are more confident about the year ahead. Our businesses have—before and since September 11—proven to be quite resilient. Despite a negative impact on sales in September, historically our biggest month, revenue from continuing operations rose 11 percent to $952 million EBITDA grew 14 percent to $142 million. We believe this is due to the value our clients place on good advice, the payoff of good investments, making value and relevance our priorities and changing our cost structure to deliver consistent growth and predictable profits.

PREDICTABLE PROFITS It was clear to us last February that the technology boom was weakening and the economy would follow. We took immediate strong action to change our cost structure yet maintain our record of growth. We divested non-performing businesses most prominently TechRepublic. We decreased staff by approximately 8 percent, lowering operating expenses by about $40 million. From being a company accustomed to driving high growth with high investment, we turned toward consistent growth and higher and more predictable profit through moderated investment. Our financial health, measured primarily by 14 percent annual growth in EBITDA, is testament to how well that strategy is working.

THE DURABILITY OF GOOD ADVICE Our prospects remain strong in fiscal 2002 for the simple reason that our clients need what we offer: practical advice that helps them preserve their revenue and earnings. In the five boom years that have just passed, we were most often called upon to help enterprises make intelligent choices about technologies that would enable their growth strategies. Today, we are working with the same clients to help them make decisions about how to evaluate cost and investment, strengthen and renegotiate relationships with suppliers, maximize the productivity of their technology, and prepare for the rebound with smart deployment strategies. While IT investments show little or no growth in 2002, they will nevertheless account for about 57 percent of all capital spending and 6 percent of GDP in the United States. Even companies cutting costs dramatically are still spending more on IT than they were two years ago. Each of them needs advice—on how to spend $1 million to earn $5 million, on how to avoid spending $5 million and remain competitive, on how to extract the greatest value from their existing assets. Gartner is better equipped and better positioned than any other company in the world to provide exactly that advice.

INVESTMENTS PAYING OFF During the past two years, we made a number of significant investments to sustain our lead as the world's top research and advisory firm. Some of those investments were unpopular because they reduced earnings-per-share. Today, they are paying dividends. We put in place a global infrastructure that enables us to manage a billion-dollar company. The result: the financial and human resource capabilities

Gartner

3

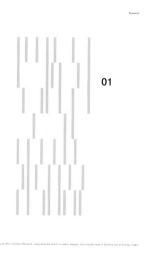

01

3. Gartner 2001 Annual Report.
Creative director: Bill Cahan.
Art directors: Bill Cahan, Bob Dinetz.
Designer: Bob Dinetz. Photographer: Frank Schwere.
Illustrator: Steve Hussey. Copywriters:
Tony Leighton, David Stolberg, Bob Dinetz.

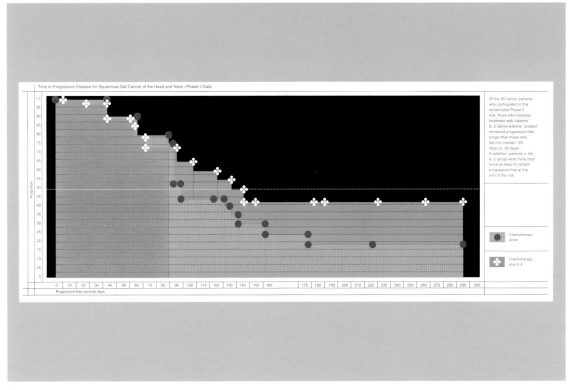

4

4. Valentis 2001 Annual Report.
Creative director: Bill Cahan.
Art directors: Bill Cahan, Sharrie Brooks.
Designer: Sharrie Brooks.
Photographer: Todd Hido.
Copywriter: Bennet Weintraub.

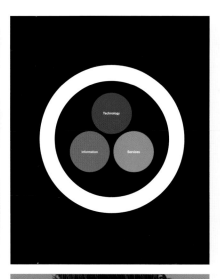

5

"Neoforma
Market Intelligence
from HPIS is the
industry standard for
accurate, third-party,
non-biased data.
My team utilizes this
data on a daily basis
for customer reviews
and tracking."

5. Neoforma 2002 Annual Report.
Creative director: Bill Cahan.
Art directors: Bill Cahan, Michael Braley.
Designer: Michael Braley.
Photographer: Jock McDonald.
Copywriter: Kathy Cooper Parker.

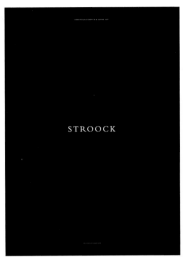

STROOCK

fling

suit

6

6. Stroock & Stroock & Lavan, LLP
Business Review Brochure.
Creative director: Bill Cahan.
Art directors: Bill Cahan, Michael Braley.
Designer: Michael Braley.
Photographer: Various.

STROOCK ZEUM

 jstar

NEKTAR GVO

 pottery barn kids

Top, from left to right:
Stroock, Stroock & Lavan, LLP
Narada Productions
ZEUM
GoBizGo
Foundry Square
jstar Brands LLC
Nektar Therapeutics, Inc.
Tumbleweed Communications
GVO
A Home Within
Pottery Barn Kids
NewEnergy

CRAWFORD/MIKUS d e s i g n
King Plow Arts Center
887 W. Marietta Street, Suite T-101
Atlanta, GA 30318
404.875.7753
www.crawfordmikus.com

CRAWFORD/MIKUS d e s i g n

At the core of Crawford/Mikus Design is the energetic husband-wife team of Elizabeth Crawford and Scott Mikus. This dynamic team has built an exceptional communications design firm that offers clients a strong balance of creative skill grounded by rock-solid strategic planning.

The company office is located in one of Atlanta's most interesting, innovative areas, a fine art and commercial art district filled with converted 19th century factories and warehouses on West Marietta Street. The building that houses Crawford/Mikus was once used to make plows and other farming machinery. In a sense, the work inside the building is the same today: a place where people like Beth, Scott, and the Crawford/Mikus team mine the fertile fields of their imaginations.

Over the past 15 years, Crawford/Mikus has created an enviable portfolio of creative work while serving an equally respectable roster of Fortune 500 clients. What drives the success of Crawford/Mikus is its combination of creative skill, rock-solid strategic thinking and unquestionable character. It is a balance few firms can boast.

A Strong Partner

- CMD's thinking is fresh, effective and tightly targeted.

- CMD's specialty is comprehensive, integrated branding systems, demonstrated by the numerous, nationally recognizable branding programs in their portfolio.

- CMD's strength is its experience in developing and migrating communications over multiple mediums, from print to web to interactive. CMD believes in parallel marketing – connected communications produce greater knowledge and perceived value of the brand as a whole among customers and employees.

- CMD's character is validated by the high percentage of repeat customers.

Clients today look for effective strategic partners who can offer the perfect balance of creative and strategic thinking. When they can also find an agency that offers a wealth of experience and unquestionable integrity, those same clients are ensured of a partner that they can rely on for years to come. Crawford/Mikus Design is that kind of place.

1. An executive level seminar campaign for NCR, a consumer data warehousing technology company, held at Chateau Elan – a world class winery, golf, and spa resort. Campaign included direct mailers, web support, signage, collateral, and packaging.

1

2

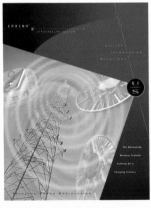

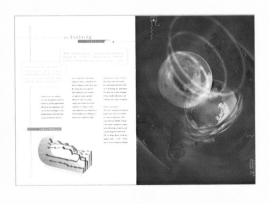

2. Brand identity for UIS, an
application development
company for energy suppliers
and distributors. Rollout
included identity and collateral
development, direct mail, website,
trade booths, and electronic
presentation materials.

1

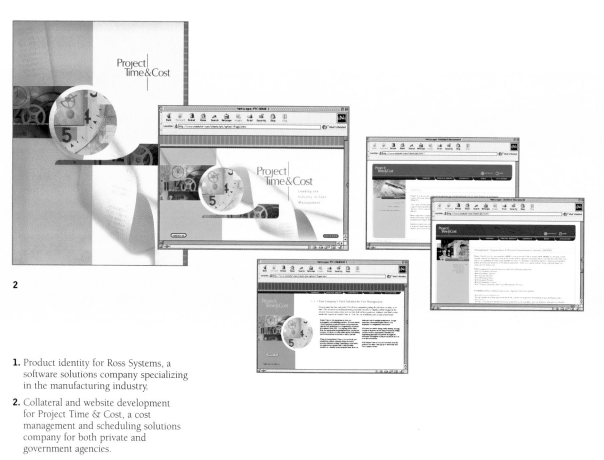

2

1. Product identity for Ross Systems, a
software solutions company specializing
in the manufacturing industry.

2. Collateral and website development
for Project Time & Cost, a cost
management and scheduling solutions
company for both private and
government agencies.

1. Brand identity for Innovative Healthcare Solutions, a healthcare IS planning, implementation and management company for healthcare organizations. Rollout included corporate identity, marketing collateral, and website development.

1

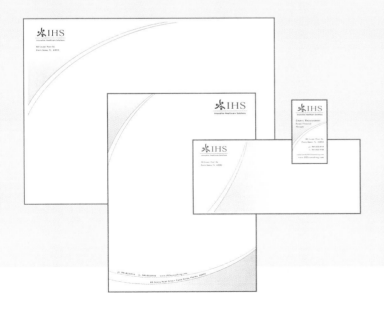

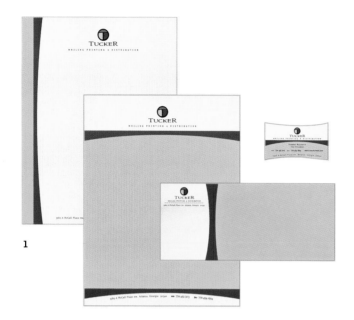

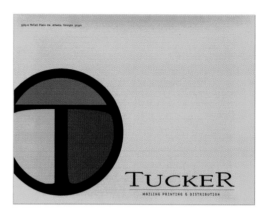

1. Logotype and identity for Tucker Mail, a full-service mail distribution company.

2. Employee Benefits Enrollment campaign for CIBA Ag, a company that designs products to enhance the performance of agricultural products.

1. Brand identity for McKessonHBOC, a software and services provider for the healthcare industry. Brand development included corporate and product collateral, trade booths, packaging, investor relations, direct mail, publications, employee communications, and guideline development.

1

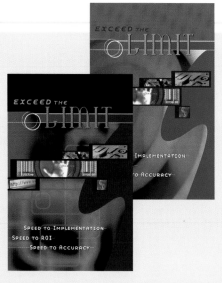

1

1. Two-phase direct mail campaign, and supporting web presence for Logility, a provider of supply chain management software.

Logos

2. Capitol Litho: Pre-press filmhouse.

3. Innovative Healthcare Solutions: An information systems and services provider for healthcare organizations.

4. Coca-Cola Fountain: Account partnership awareness campaign.

5. Clearly Atlanta International: A non-profit organization creatively promoting international culture and arts in Atlanta.

6. Craig Bromley: Photographer.

7. World Vibe: A non-profit organization taking an untraditional approach to showcasing international visual and performing artists.

2

3

4

5

6

7

CREATIVILLE, INC.

Creativille, Inc.
1905 Marconi Avenue
Creativille, MO 63110

314.862.6270 voice
314.727.1928   fax
postoffice@creativille.net

www.creativille.net

Be Simple. Be Passionate. Be Creative.

Creativille is located in the heartland of the U.S. – in St. Louis, Missouri to be exact. Specializing in corporate communications his entire career, Steve Hartman operates Creativille as a firm specializing in financial, employee and strategic communication and brand design. Most of the communication problems that Creativille solves are directly with executive level departments of mid- to large-sized corporations and evolve around improving the corporate brand image.

Be Simple. Be Passionate. Be Creative. Creativille's mantra was developed from Steve's own persona. Believing that the process of design is from the brain and heart of a designer, Steve operates Creativille around what he believes are three of his top character attributes. Communicating and relationships go hand-in-hand, and these three characteristics foster success.

Be Simple. Simple doesn't mean bland, and simple isn't always easy. Simple is well-received. Simple design. Simple process. Simple to understand. Simple is a goal when complexity is present, yet not welcome. The design process isn't easy, and Creativille's clients know it... that's why they go to Creativille...to keep it simple.

Be Passionate. Love what you do, and you'll do it well. Design is Creativille's passion. They love it. They adore it. They read, write and talk about it everyday. It may be a little obsessive at times, but it shows in Creativille's work. Not bad... pretty good, actually.

Be Creative. Always. Not just in the solution, but in the process, as well. Creativity is fueled by curiosity. Inspiration, invention and imagination are what's behind Creativille's creativity. Heck, its in the name, it better be.

1

2

1. Helzberg Diamonds' 2001 Annual Report
*"The Spirit Inside" focuses on the "Brand" of
Helzberg Diamonds and its impact on its people,
product and position in the marketplace.*

2. Helzberg Diamonds' 2000 Annual Report
*"Generations" focuses on the heritage of excellent
relationships with its clientele, community and
employees.*

3. Helzberg Diamonds Masterpiece™
Brand Identity and Packaging
*This rare loose diamond product was named
and designed to match its heirloom potential and
high-quality character. The new rare and high-quality
loose diamond product is packaged in this high-touch
heirloom dossier along with its certificate of
authenticity, educational brochure and data card.*

5. Helzberg Diamonds' Guarantee system
*The visual brand of Helzberg Diamonds is extended
in this post-sale literature.*

6. Helzberg Diamond Heritage Timeline
*The heritage of Helzberg Diamonds goes home with
each visitor from a Helzberg Diamonds store in this
new and existing market positioning tool.*

Helzberg
diamond masterpiece

3

4

5

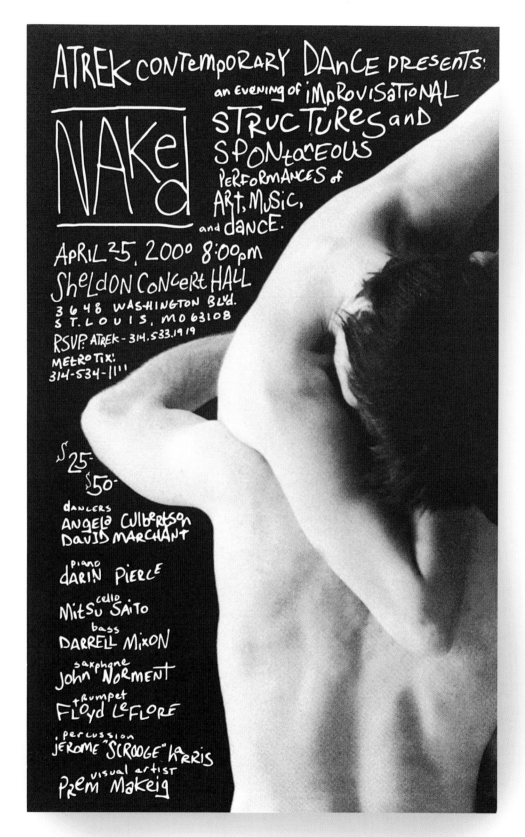

2

4

Pro-Bono Posters

1. Atrek Dance Poster
This dance company poster was created to promote the spontaneous, improvised and raw performance of "Naked," and has become an identity for the same performance each year.

2. Belle, Poster for Cause
This poster is the first of a series of limited-edition signed art prints promoting various causes.

3. AIGA Vote Poster
Part of a national campaign, this poster encourages the public to vote by celebrating independence and unity through a compelling illustration and George Washington quote.

2

May Department Stores Company

1. Executive College Recruiting program
This extensive program was designed to bring a common approach to a multiple brand corporation in its national college recruiting effort. This multi-piece system actually simplifies what was previous designed.

2. May Foundation philanthropy ad campaign
Designed to fill fundraising event journal space, this campaign carries the brand and corporate messages to its charities of choice.

3. May Board of Directors Meeting Materials
This year in Napa Valley, the board of directors held there planning meeting. Meeting materials, as well as, welcoming kits and invitations were designed to add to the professional experience.

3

1

2

3

4

1. MasterCard International Intranet Campaign
   This internal campaign was created to launch the new employee intranet "PeoplePlace," a site dedicated to accessing and updating personal employee information and work history.

2. International Truck Campaign Calendar
   For the launch of new model trucks, parts inventory, training materials and ad campaign, this internal calendar was designed to be posted at dealer sites across North America.

3. HOK Process Archive
   Five three-volume books were produced to archive the process of designing and building the Northwest Memorial Hospital in Chicago, IL.

4. KDG Anniversary Promotions
   The year 2000 marked the 25 year anniversary for Kuhlmann Design Group, an architecture and engineering firm. A new year's card, wine and champaign bottles, and other premium items were produced to celebrate both the new year and anniversary.

decker design

14 West 23rd Street
New York, NY 10010
212.633.8588
www.deckerdesign.com

Effective design
moves product,
inspires people
and builds brands.

At Decker Design we work with our clients
to help them see their communication challenges from a different perspective.

Each assignment, regardless of the size and
scope of the project, is approached with
a disciplined strategic process. We research
a company, product or service in relation
to the end user or marketplace. Our experience, instinct and insight enable us to ask
the right questions to establish a foundation
of relevant knowledge. We understand that
information doesn't gain power until placed
in a context: our strength is contextualizing
knowledge as it relates to business objectives
and identifying a key leverage point. This
leverage point individualizes strategy and its
creative development, resulting in a solution
that is unique.

It is our process that differentiates us and
informs each of our services. Combined with
hard work and responsiveness, we build
integrated, visionary and targeted branding
programs and marketing communications
in industries from architecture to financial
services and everything in between.

decker design

AIGA

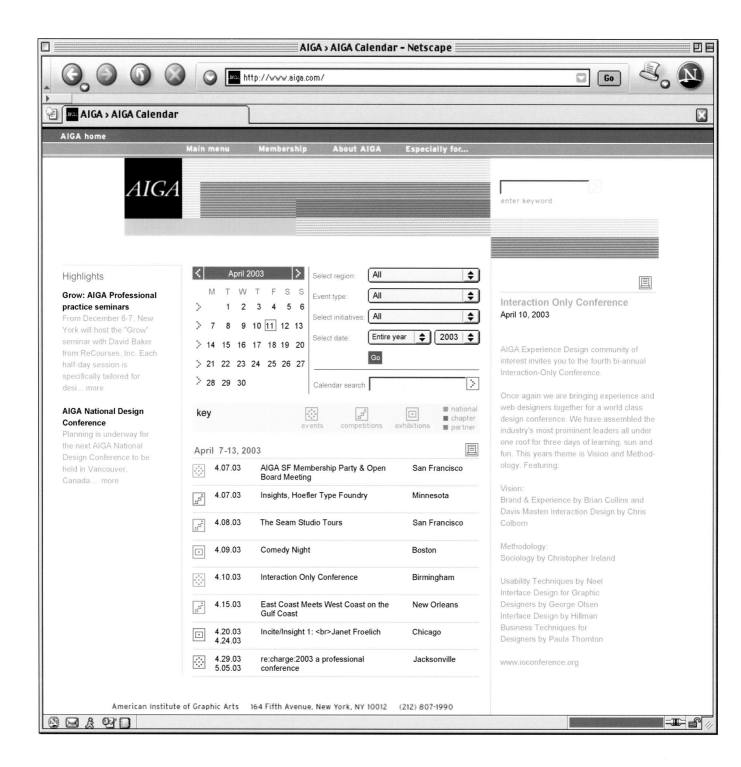

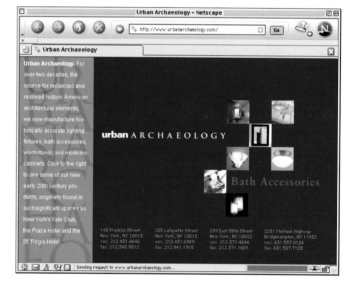

KNOLL

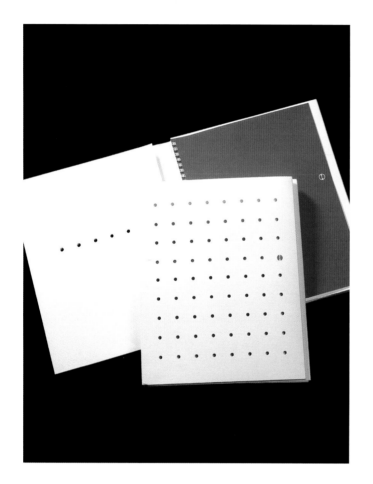

THE CITIGROUP PRIVATE BANK

PSEG

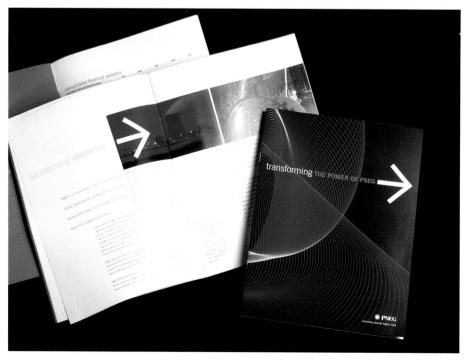

URS

MUTUAL OF AMERICA

HOLIDAY CARDS

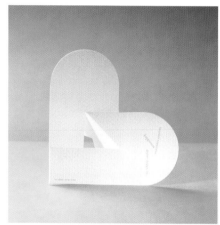

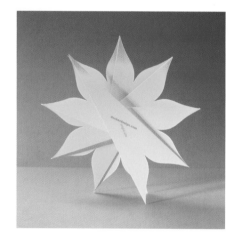
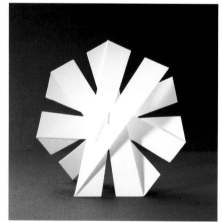
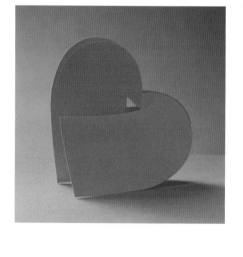

Dever Designs
1056 West Street
Laurel, Maryland 20707
Telephone: 301-776-2812
Fax: 301-953-1196
www.deverdesigns.com

dever designs

Good design is the result of careful listening, creative problem-solving and artistic execution. It is the point where art and communication meet. On that premise Dever Designs was founded in 1985 as a multi-disciplinary design group. Located in the suburbs of Washington D.C. we primarily serve clients in the mid-Atlantic region, however our award-winning design and penchant for exceptional client service have attracted a loyal clientele across North America.

At Dever Designs we believe that effective design is quality design. Design that will work hard for you and your organization. We enter into a partnership with each of our clients to create strategically conceived dynamic materials that clearly project your image and communicate your message to your intended audience.

As a multi-disciplinary studio Dever Designs' talented staff offers a full array of services. While we focus on brand identification and publication design our portfolio and client list are varied and diverse. This wide range of projects have earned Dever Designs over 350 major design awards for excellence and more importantly a loyal clientele.

How can Dever Designs serve you?

1

2

1. Family Therapy Networker magazines
   and Symposium poster

2. National Museum for Women in
   the Arts magazine

3. Government Windows NT magazine

4. Glencoe Literature Library book covers

5. Physician Assistant Foundation logo

6. Diamanti logo

7. Museum conference logo

8. Institutional Reform and the Informal
   Sector logo

DIAMANTI

6

7

iris

8

1. Dever Designs series of promotional cards
2. Number Six Software brochure
3. Martin's Fine Furniture logo
4. Development Alternatives, Inc. logo
5. Illinois Conference of Seventh-Day Adventist logo

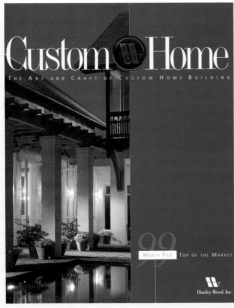

6. Hanley-Wood media kit

7. National Fish & Wildlife Foundation 2001 annual report

8. American Gas Association logo

Dever Designs

1

3

2

1-3. Front Porch magazine brand identity: website, magazine covers and department icons

4. Library of Congress / James Madison Council Commemorative Book

5. Series of ads for Independent Bankers Association of America

1. Melwood Exhibit
2. Dever Designs self-promotion brochure
3. Fullbleed magazine

1

2

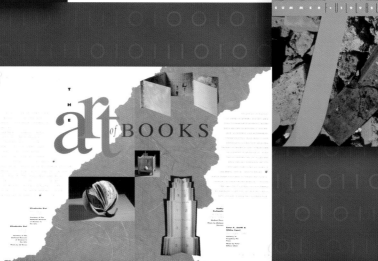

3

DUPUIS

877.854.8700

info@dupuisgroup.com

www.dupuisgroup.com

OFFICES

Los Angeles • Chicago

New York • Germany

DUPUIS

Connecting People with Brands.

That's the bottom line of strategic design; understanding not just how customers behave but why they behave that way.

Customers connect to brands as they do to their friends – through common interests, values and lifestyle. They seek out those that are fun to be with, that make them feel good about themselves.

From a first-hand examination of how your buyers experience your brand in the marketplace, we create an identity that successfully speaks to them, even in a crowded retail environment.

We create identities, packaging and personalities for brands and products ranging from food and beverage to the life sciences – forging a successful link between people and brands.

Archway

Bed & Breakfast

Crispy Classics

packaging program

Kellogg's

Pop-Tarts brand revitalization

& packaging system

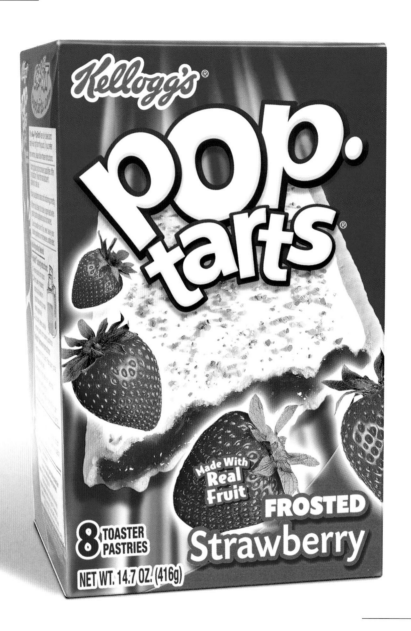

Kellogg's

Cereal & Milk Bars

packaging

Keebler

Zesta branding &

packaging revitalization

Foster Farms

Coastal Range Organics

branding for a line of

fresh chicken products

Acco Brands

Swingline architecture,

structure & packaging

VanKind Foods

Above & Beyond branding

& packaging for a soy-based

cream cheese product line

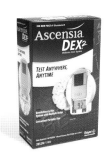

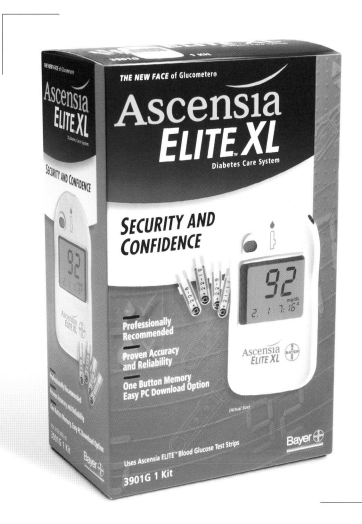

Topz Restaurant

branding, environmental graphics

& identity system

622 Third Avenue
New York, NY 10017
212.905.7200
212.515.7700
Contact:
hlevin@frankfurtbalkind.com

FRANKFURT BALKIND

Every company has a story.

Sometimes that story is out of date. Sometimes it's too broad. Sometimes it's too narrow or not narrow enough. Sometimes it just misses.

When it's time to consider change, companies come to Frankfurt Balkind for help.

We work to clarify who you are . . . focus and define your messages . . . and, if needed, create a new name or a new identity to help you communicate. Then, we help you extend your story in a way that resonates with audiences coherently across all touch points.

Depending upon a company's need, we work in three phases:

Phase One focuses on analysis and development of the underpinnings for "The Strategic Idea," which shapes beliefs, behavior and actions, driving internal cultures while sustaining customer relationships.

Phase Two centers on developing "The Brand Platform," which provides the building blocks that transform The Strategic Idea into a tangible blueprint for the company. This may be comprised of: a Positioning Statement, Message Architecture, Name and Nomenclature, Graphic Identity, Brand Relationships, and System Guidelines.

Phase Three utilizes different media forms to "Tell The Story." Effective storytelling requires an understanding of how the basic building blocks of the company can be brought together to leverage the virtues of each medium. Whether a web site, marketing communications, internal communications, environments or an advertising campaign, we reinforce the core idea without creating an overly complex, rigid cookie-cutter that can undercut the ability to tell a compelling story.

Since 1972, we've worked with literally hundreds of companies, from global giants to intriguing start-ups, helping co-author their stories and bring them to life.

The following pages visually demonstrate some of the results.

1

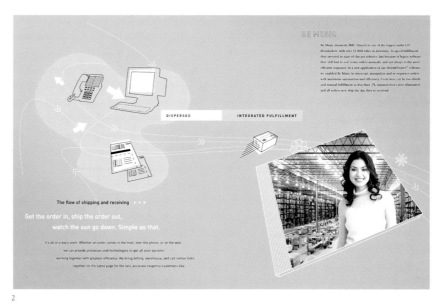

2

3

4

PITNEY BOWES Misperceived as a mail meter company, Pitney Bowes has undergone a new worldwide branding initiative. We've worked to develop more accurate positioning – as partners critical to engineering an organization's mail and document flow.
1, 2) Annual Report, **3, 4**) Communication Chain Management Brochure directed to the C-Suite, **5,7**) Headquarter's Exhibit, **6, 8**) pitneybowes.com.

Pitney Bowes

5

6

7

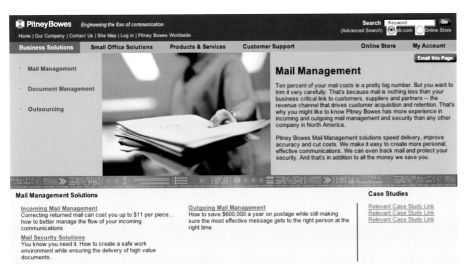

8

TOTAL MERRILL^{SM}

1

2

TOTAL MERRILL Against a backdrop of a down-market and consumer skepticism, we launched Total Merrill, a new approach to wealth management that ties together Merrill Lynch's breadth and depth of services in a holistic way for high net worth clients. Along with working to develop the brand message architecture, brand identity and its guidelines, we created **1,2**) the Global Private Client Website, and **3,4**) the Introductory Micro-site.

3

4

1

TAPESTRIA Owned by global wall-covering giant Hunter Douglas, Tapestria.com is a unique destination for designers to browse and buy fabrics and rugs — direct for the first time — from the world's best mills. We partnered with Tapestria and their pr firm R/F Binder to reach their image-conscious audience through creating: **1**) Catalogues, **2**) Advertising, **3**) Tapestria.com rug area (and home page), and **4**) Direct Mail.

2

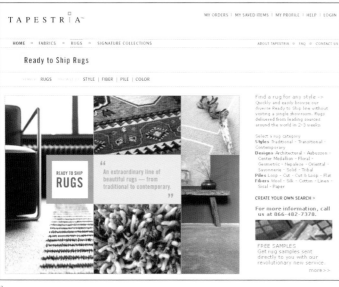

3

4

TAPESTRIA™

A Hunter Douglas Company

Griffith Phillips Creative, Inc.
10000 North Central Expressway
Suite 1350
Dallas, Texas 75231
214.265.0026
Fax: 214.265.0189
info@gpcreative.com
www.gpcreative.com

GRIFFITH PHILLIPS CREATIVE

At GPC, we have a simple approach to advertising and design. We listen to our clients' needs. We learn their business. We create smart solutions that make an impact. And, most importantly, we deliver real-world results. It's a simple philosophy. But one that has garnered much success, both for GPC and our clients.

We're not just an ad agency. We're a partner.

At GPC, we don't view ourselves as just another advertising agency. We like to think of ourselves as an extension of your marketing department. We listen to your needs. Then we get down to work. Planning. Strategizing. Creating. All the while, making sure that you are included in every stage of the game. That's what the GPC philosophy is all about. And it's why – for over a decade now – we have successfully developed thousands of strategic, insightful and compelling marketing messages for hundreds of satisfied clients.

Let's just say we wear a lot of hats.

Yes, we're a full-service advertising agency, which means we do it all. Print. Collateral. Broadcast. Direct mail. Outdoor. But we offer additional services too – like interactive communications, brand identity, trade show support, corporate videos, package design and Flash-based communications. Just to name a few. So whether you need a multi-layered branding campaign, a targeted B2B e-business initiative or anything in between, you've come to the right place.

Sit back. Relax. Enjoy the scenery.

Now that you know a little bit about us, go ahead and take a look at our portfolio. It's just a small sample of our work, but we think it clearly demonstrates our creative prowess, our range of experience and our passion for developing quality work.

1. Daisytek 2001 Annual Report
2. Verizon ESG Capabilities Brochure
3. HQ VoiceWorks Direct Mail
4. TU Communications Collateral
5. Dallas Ad League TOPS Call For Entries
6. GTE Telops Brochure
7. Nortel Networks Supervision Brochure
8. Daisytek 2002 Annual Report

1

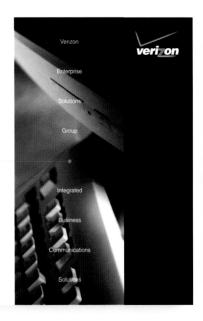

2

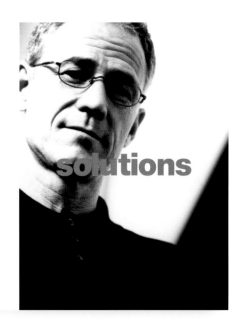

3

4

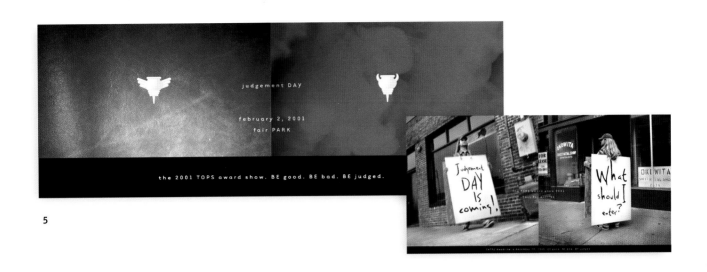

5

6

7

8

1

2

1. Datamax of Texas Sales Proposal
2. GTE Forum Magazine
3. 9/11 Memorial Poster
4. Lennox Corporate Brochure
5. Lennox Lobby Displays

3

4

5

1

2

3

4

5

6

7

8

9

1. Craig Varjabedian Photography
4. Datamax of Texas
7. TXU Custom Solutions

2. Spina Bifida Association of Dallas
5. HQ VoiceWorks
8. SureThought

3. GTE Power Path
6. GTE Intelligate
9. Sprint Image Source

1

2

3

1. Greater Dallas Salvation Army
   2002 Annual Report
2. Sprint Internet Guide
3. Nortel Networks
   CallPilot Brochure
4. BenefitMall Welcome Kit
5. BenefitMall Ad
6. iXP Corp. Ad
7. CTX Mortgage Ad
8. TXU Communications Newspaper Ads
9. Verizon ESG Ad
10. Datamax of Texas Ad

4

Why on earth would you give me my very own free home page?

BenefitMall.com

To get your free broker home page,
visit the all new www.benefitmall.com/freeweb today.

5

I EXPECT LEADERSHIP.

I EXPECT RESPONSIVENESS.

I EXPECT INTEGRATED TECHNOLOGIES.

I EXPECT CONTINUITY OF OPERATIONS.

I EXPECT SUCCESS.

EXPECT SUCCESS.

6

**Do one thing.
And do it well.**

At CTX, our thing is mortgage lending.

7

Guess what Mom?
Trevor had his first plane ride today.

They've giggled on the phone together every Tuesday
for the last 47 years. Some things never change.

TXU

www.txucom.com

TXU Communications

8

Verizon Enterprise Solutions

One company. A world of networking solutions. Verizon.

Take a closer look at Verizon Enterprise Solutions, and you'll be amazed at what you'll find. A proven company with more
than 80 years of industry experience. A complete portfolio of end-to-end networking products and services. And the people
who can help customize a solution that's right for your business. It's all here. And it's changing the face of enterprise networking.

verizon.com/enterprisesolutions

verizon

9

○ Document outsourcing
○ Digital imaging
○ Information technology
○ Facilities management
○ Color graphics
● All of the above

For those of you who believe "All of the above" is
a perfectly acceptable answer. Meet Datamax.

datamax

10

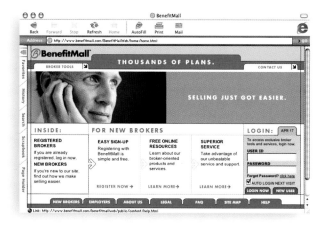

1

2

3

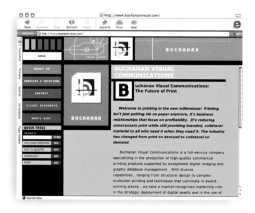

4

1. BenefitMall Website
2. Datamax of Texas Website
3. Spina Bifida Association of Dallas Website
4. Buchanan Visual Communications Website
5. Verizon Logistics Interactive Catalog
6. iXP Corp. Website

5

6

Photo by Maxwell Balmain Photography

HORNALL ANDERSON DESIGN WORKS

Since opening our doors over twenty years ago, Hornall Anderson Design Works has successfully connected companies to their customers by designing experiences that define the spirit, soul and value of their brand. Through intelligent strategy, emotional design and interactive development, we deliver results that work. The diverse creative experience and expertise of our employees helps build a thriving working environment that fosters meaningful connections between people, ideas and technology.

In a marketplace of constantly changing brand images and messages, we create a unique freshness in each design, allowing our clients to distinguish themselves amongst their competitors. By blending the creative and business disciplines of our firm, we develop responsible, integral relationships that continuously stand the test of time.

Hornall Anderson specializes in brand and communications strategy; traditional brand design, including identity, packaging and literature systems; integrated online design, including motion graphics and interactive media; information architecture; web development and branded retail environments.

1008 Western Avenue
Suite 600
Seattle, Washington 98104
P: 206.467.5800
www.hadw.com

Hornall Anderson Design Works, Inc.

1 Orivo identity for a firm that helps companies deliver exciting, innovative products to the public. While generating ideas for new products, this company also matches brands with market opportunities and speeds the product to market.

2 Pacific Raceways identity for an organization providing tracks for recreational auto racing.

3 Otoño Plaza identity for an innovative business park providing a retail and professional environment.

4 Nordstrom Salad Dressing packaging available in an upscale retailer's café and bistro venue.

5 Stanley Vacuum Bottle packaging for insulated, portable beverage containers.

6 Orivo brochure for a firm that helps companies deliver exciting, innovative products to the public. While generating ideas for new products, this company also matches brands with market opportunities and speeds the product to market.

7 Pacific Raceways stationery program for an organization providing tracks for recreational auto racing.

ORIV●

1

2

OTOÑO
PLAZA

3

4

5

6

7

8   InSite Works identity for a
    full-spectrum, architectural
    design firm.

9   TruckTrax identity for an
    automated, truck tracking
    system designed for the
    ready-mix industry fleet.

10 FreeMotion identity for a
    manufacturer of strength
    and cardio-fitness machines.

11 InSite Works stationery for a
    full-spectrum, architectural
    design firm.

12 OneWorld Challenge promo-
    tional merchandise for a
    Seattle-based racing yacht in
    the 2003 America's Cup.

13 Big Island Candies "Olive
    Oil" cookie packaging
    designed for a Hawaii-based,
    confections retailer.

14 FreeMotion brochure for
    a manufacturer of strength
    and cardio-fitness machines.

8

9

11

12

13

14

1 Lincoln Square identity for the retail component of an upscale, urban, mixed-use real estate project.

2 Erickson McGovern identity for an architectural firm specializing in school designs.

3 Hornall Anderson Design Works identity for a branding, graphic and web site design firm.

4 Seattle SuperSonics postcards for direct mail and marketing use by a NBA basketball team.

5 Seattle SuperSonics 2003/2004 ticket books for a NBA basketball team's season ticket holders.

6 Seattle SuperSonics 2003/2004 subscriber brochure for a NBA basketball team's season ticket holders.

7 Seattle SuperSonics sales folder for direct marketing and promotions of a NBA basketball team.

8 Seattle SuperSonics sales brochures promoting special ticket packages for a NBA basketball team.

1

2

3

4

5

6

7

8

9 Attenex identity for a manufacturer of data forensics
software.

10 aQuantive identity for a
holding company of digital
marketing firms.

11 Nordstrom RACK identity
for a reduced-price, upscale,
retail shopping complex.

12 Nordstrom RACK exterior
signage for a reduced-price,
upscale, retail shopping
complex.

13 Tend Blends packaging for
a manufacturer and retailer
of a holistic system of bath
and body products.

14 Tend Blends packaging for
a manufacturer and retailer
of a holistic system of bath
and body products.

15 Boullioun Aviation Services
2002 annual report for the
third largest aircraft leasing
company in the world.

aQuantive

9   10   11

12

13

14

15

1 AT&T Wireless mMode Flash demo serving as an interactive explanation of a communication company's newest wireless service. Individual vignettes—each focusing on a specific feature of the phone—were created in story-telling fashion as a user-friendly means of showcasing this new service.

2 Weyerhaeuser corporate web site for an international company with a diverse natural products offering. This site needed to be expandable to include the many business segments of Weyerhaeuser and convey a company-wide set of values. It also emphasizes the client's commitment to growth and renewal, as well as their long and rich history.

3 Weyerhaeuser Realty Investors (WRI) web site for a company serving as a reliable and flexible equity source for quality residential builders. This site serves as an extension of WRI's corporate brochure, and is intended to communicate authenticity, honesty, a strong foundation and heritage, trust and careful innovation.

1

2

3

4   F5 Networks CD demo for a
    service provider of Internet
    traffic control and content
    management applications.
    It was designed specifically
    to be utilized as a sales tool.
    The new demo was then
    placed on the F5 corporate
    site, a product launch site,
    incorporated on a product
    launch CD and employed
    by the sales team to launch
    PowerPoint presentations.

5   K2 Corporation web site
    for a manufacturer of snow
    skis, snow boards, skates,
    and bikes. Fun graphics and
    amusing descriptions make
    the selection process enter-
    taining, while still supplying
    the browser with helpful
    information.

6   LifeSpan BioSciences web
    site for a bio-tech company
    that uses a patent-pending
    technology to target genes
    for drug research and devel-
    opment. One of the main
    conceptual goals was to
    bring to light the intersection
    of humanity with their
    deeply scientific work, there-
    by placing their technical
    content into a context that
    enables visitors to better
    relate.

7   Mahlum Architects web site
    for a Seattle, WA-based
    architectural design firm.
    Since it is Mahlum's belief
    that architecture can be both
    intuitive and rational, poetic
    and mathematical, this phase
    two of their site examines
    the left-brained side of their
    company and provides a
    counterpoint to the existing
    intuitive side.

8   Orivo web site for a firm that
    helps companies deliver
    exciting, innovative products
    to the public. While generat-
    ing ideas for new products,
    this company also matches
    brands with market opportu-
    nities and speeds the product
    to market.

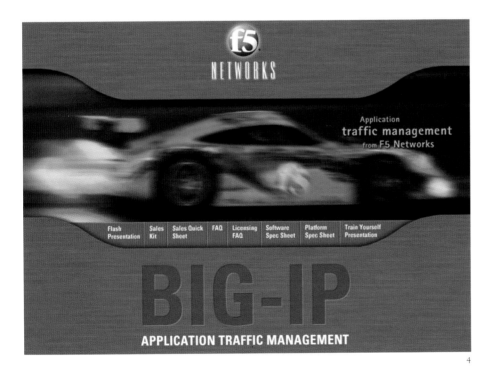

4

5

6

7

8

1   Active Wear identity for a trade-based, textile company which manufactures fleece material for retail clothing and automotive upholstering companies.

2   Solavie identity for a Sun Valley, ID-based spa retreat and manufacturer of natural spa products for skin and hair treatments.

3   Pace International identity for a manufacturer of cleaners and coatings, which are applied to fruits and vegetables during packing.

4   Nordstrom Chocolate Buttons candy packaging for sale in an upscale retailer's café and bistro venue.

5   Mahlum Architects corporate brochure for a Seattle, WA-based architectural design firm.

6   Sticky Fingers Bakery "Scone Mix" packaging for a high-quality, gift catalog retailer.

7   Widmer Brothers "Drop Top" Amber Ale packaging for a Portland, OR-based brewery and distributor of micro-brewed beverages.

1

2

3

4

5

6

7

Hull Creative Group
667 Boylston Street
Boston, MA 02116
617-536-1017
team@hullcreative.com
www.hullcreative.com

HULL CREATIVE GROUP

BRANDING, unified collateral systems, comprehensive marketing strategies.

From our roots as a design studio providing clients with fresh ways to visually communicate with customers and their audiences, Hull Creative Group has evolved over the years to a full service firm offering design, marketing, and public relations to companies at a point of growth and change. As specialists serving the diverse needs of the business to business sector, we use our 15 years of industry expertise to help these clients most effectively reach their audiences through targeted marketing strategy and high-impact design.

Whether the goal is developing a powerful branding campaign that builds corporate identity, redesigning a Web site to add visual appeal and accessibility, or creating a memorable annual report that strengthens the company image — whatever the project, whatever its size or scope — our work is always about helping our clients meet their business goals. Our intrinsic values of respect, responsiveness and accessibility are reflected in the unsurpassable service we provide.

The combination of intelligence, originality and a passion to create the best solution possible — qualities found in each team professional — help to make Hull Creative Group a full service agency with a dynamic edge.

1

1. Circadian Technologies
Working Nights Poster
Integrated promotions create new image for
products and services.

2. Circadian Technologies
Working Nights Calendar
Joyful illustrations, accessible graphics and
stickers create a fun year-round resource for
industry work/lifestyle tips.

2

1. **Geac Computer Corporation Annual Report**
   Focuses on international brands to position company as powerful, accessible and poised for growth.

2. **Geac Computer Corporation Corporate Report**
   Active photographs and dynamic design reinforce new company brand.

1

2

1

2

3

4

1. MRO Software | Corporate Brochure
   Highlights the success of an established leader.

2. Inmagic Content Server | Product Identity

3. Kada Systems | Corporate Identity

4. Dare Family Services | Corporate Identity

1

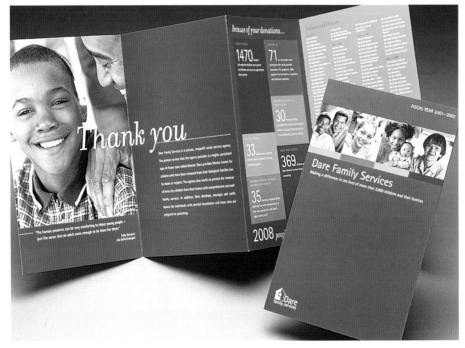

2

3

1. **MRO Software | Annual Report**
   Reinforces the sophistication and consistency
   of the corporate brand.

2. **Dare Family Services | Annual Report**
   Functions as both year in review and annual
   appeal.

3. **Dare Family Services | Letterhead**
   Integrated collateral system designed to
   upgrade image and heighten visibility.

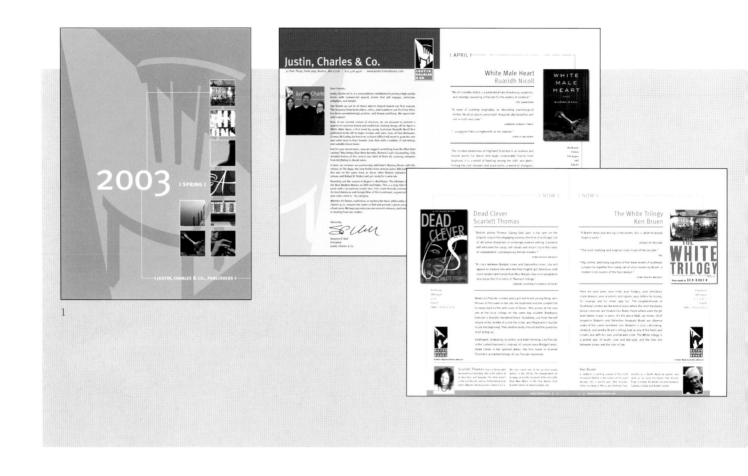

1

1. **Justin, Charles & Co. | Spring 2003 catalog**
   Vibrant catalog designed to introduce publisher
   and first year titles as welcomed additions to
   the literary scene.

2. **Justin, Charles & Co. | Web site**
   Launches edgy new publisher's brand with
   sophisticated colors, clearly defined categories
   and easy navigation.

3. **Massachusetts Department of
   Environmental Management
   Annual Report**

4. **Boston Harbor Islands | Web site**
   Accommodates massive amounts of information,
   geared toward three distinct audiences,
   while featuring easy navigation and great
   visual appeal.

3

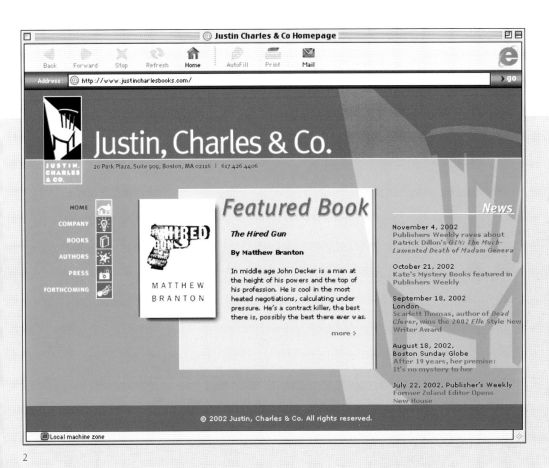

2

4

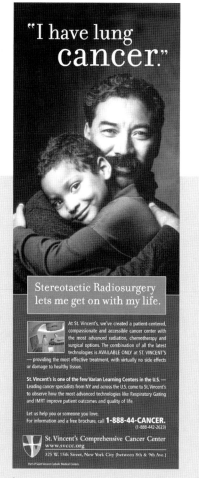

1. Summit Press | Mailer
Bold photographs and vivid colors promote
new printing techniques.

**2. St. Vincent's Comprehensive Cancer Center
Advertisements**
Positions cancer center as compassionate
state-of-the-art health care facility.

3. Allyn & Bacon | Institutional Brochure
Establishes educational publisher as the
premier choice for prospective authors.

Kolar Design Inc.
2134 Alpine Place
Cincinnati, Ohio 45206
p 513.241.4884
f 513.241.2240
www.kolardesign.net

KOLAR DESIGN INC.

Kolar Design is a premier visual communications and architectural graphic design studio specializing in wayfinding systems, identity development and environmental design. Since its inception in 1989, KD has been providing an innovative, multi-disciplinary approach to concept design, development and implementation to a diverse mix of clients.

Whether working for a Fortune 500 company, a university, a hospital, or a city, Kolar Design and its team of graphic, industrial and environmental designers brings a systematic approach to creating seamless, memorable and effective solutions that span the two-dimensional and three-dimensional disciplines. Kolar Design's fifteen creative professionals become closely involved with each client, seeking out their unique values, aspirations, needs and priorities, discovering the narrative landscape and the vocabulary of each project. In short, Kolar Design captures the spirit of each project and the essence of each environment.

But that's not enough. It is Kolar Design's unparalleled strength as a collaborative design firm that allows for the highest quality solution. KD works in collaboration – from design through fabrication – with planners, architects, landscape architects, engineers, industrial designers and fabricators. KD has worked with dozens of cities, universities and villages to establish unique urban district identities. Kolar Design has facilitated public workshops and interactive sessions to create consensus and excitement for its numerous private and public sector projects.

Clients return time and time again to Kolar Design for environmental and architectural graphics, systems development, wayfinding, computer aided visualization, design-related branding and large scale event system design. Kolar Design creates lasting relationships because they create spaces, places and visual identities that stay in our memory; because they solve visual communication and architectural graphic design problems collaboratively, with integrity, while honoring design, harmony and aesthetics.

Theodore M. Berry International Friendship Park, Cincinnati, Ohio

design team: **Kolar Design, Siebert Design** landscape architects: **EDAW, Human Nature** architect: **Fearing & Hagenauer** fabricator: **Geograph Industries**

1.

2.

3.

4.

Kolar Design collaborated with landscape architects to develop the park's unique features, place-makers and pathways on an underutilized strip of land along the Ohio River. Named in honor of Cincinnati's first African American mayor and foreign ambassador, all of the park's features were designed to celebrate and/or punctuate the natural, linear setting and the many cultures which help make up the region, the country and the world. The largest graphic feature is the 24 foot wide entrance sculpture. The curved aluminum design features an energetic color palette as well as dimensionally lettered translations in eight different languages.

1. Park Logo
2. Friendship Flag Colonnade
3. Recognition Pylon with Identification Band and Graphic Panel
4. Entrance Sculpture with Dimensional Typography and Braid Pattern
5. Example of Regulatory Signage
6. Bronze Medallion in the Garden of Australia
7. Detail of Bronze Medallion in the Garden of Australia
8. & 9. Map of International Friendship Park
10. & 11. Details of Imprinted Concrete

5.

6.

7.

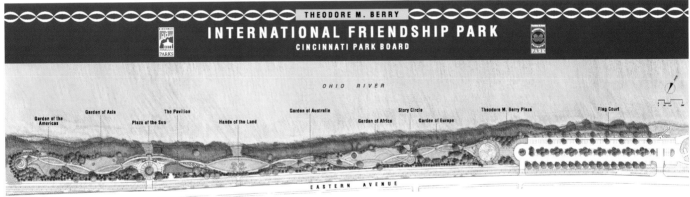

8.

9.

10.

11.

139

Cincinnati Children's Hospital Medical Center, Cincinnati, Ohio

design team: **Kolar Design, Firehouse Design, Doepke Associates** architect: **GBBN** landscape architect: **Doepke Associates** fabricator: **Geograph Industries, ArtiSigns**

1.

CHMC was in great need of a comprehensive wayfinding system because of the growth of the hospital campus. The project architect spearheaded a multi-disciplinary approach to transform individual buildings into a connected city.

Exterior wayfinding sculptures reinforce the hospital's philosophy of "CARE", an interior wayfinding system assists users in navigating in stressful situations, and garage signage provides safe, clear direction and memorable parking locations for

hospital visitors and employees. The directory serves as a key to the wayfinding information hierarchy established by color, typography, form, and new nomenclature for hospital buildings, floors, and rooms.

2.

1. Overhead Interior Wayfinding Sign
2. Wall-mounted Interior Wayfinding Sign
3. Hospital Directory Sign
4. Exterior Directional Sign
5. Hospital Directory and Wayfinding Plan

3.

4.

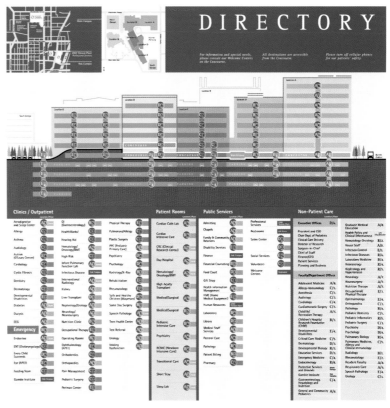

5.

Kolar Design Inc.

Allied Insurance Home Office, Des Moines, Iowa
design team: **Kolar Design** architects: **Heinlein Schrock Stearns, SVPA Architects** landscape architect: **Myers Schmalenberger** parking consultant: **Walker Parking**

3.

4.

5.

1.

2.

6.

Kolar Design developed a comprehensive sign system for the headquarters of this national insurance company. The design encompasses the home office and parking facility, each of which is connected to the city skywalk system. Sign types for the Allied Insurance Home Office campus include interior and exterior wayfinding, identification, regulatory, facilities management and specialty placemakers. KD created simple nomenclature – Central, East and West – to orient employees and visitors to the campus' two buildings and parking garage. Further, Kolar Design derived the steel and glass palette, the proportions and tactile surfaces from the architecture itself to create a seamlessly integrated wayfinding system.

7.

1. Exterior Brand Identification Sign
2. Interior Brand Identification Sign
3. Interior Room Identification Sign
4. Interior Room Identification Sign with Insert
5. Interior Regulatory Sign
6. Clock Tower Cafe Sign
7. Interior Department Identification Sign
8. Exterior Parking Garage Identification Sign
9. Parking Garage Wayfinding Sign

8.

9.

Identity Systems

Kolar Design analyzes multiple levels of information to discover the essence of each client's message, crafting it into a strong, unique and cohesive brand identity.

Kolar Design's systematic design process includes the development of marketing communications, collateral material, annual reports, event promotions and advertising.

1.

6.

7.

2.

3.

8.

9.

4.

1. Downtown Cincinnati Inc. Logo
2. JH Photo Logo
3. Architectural Foundation Logo
4. Tall Stacks Logo
5. KZF Design Logo
6. Avery Dennison Product Reference Guide
7. Downtown Cincinnati Inc. Annual Report
8. JH Photo Identity System
9. AIA Ohio Valley Region Conference System
10. KZF Design Identity System

10.

kor group

visual communications
branding
naming
print design
advertising
direct mail
web design
environmental graphics
packaging

kor group
One Design Center Place
Suite 733
Boston, MA 02210
tel: 617.330.1007
www.kor.com

SPIRITED COLLABORATION

The word "group" is part of our name for some very good reasons. Successful design doesn't happen in a vacuum – it comes from strategically integrating the best input from multiple sources. To that end, we listen actively to every member of the project team – clients, staff, principals, and creative partners – and translate those contributions into clean, colorful, high-energy design. The result is a greater sense of collective ownership among everyone involved, and an outstanding final product.

MORE BRAINPOWER

kor group is led by three highly experienced professionals: Anne Callahan, MB Jarosik, and Karen Dendy Smith. Our founding partners bring the highest standards of professionalism to creative and project management efforts, giving clients the benefit of multiple perspectives, an abundance of fresh ideas, and exceptional service.

HEAD AND HEART

More than ever before, designers' endeavors must translate into tangible results for clients that yield a return on their investment. At kor group, we balance this strategic orientation with a belief in the human value of design, and its ability to inform, motivate, and inspire. We achieve this balance by organizing kor group around the principles of passion, integrity, and focus, which have translated into a decade of success for the firm.

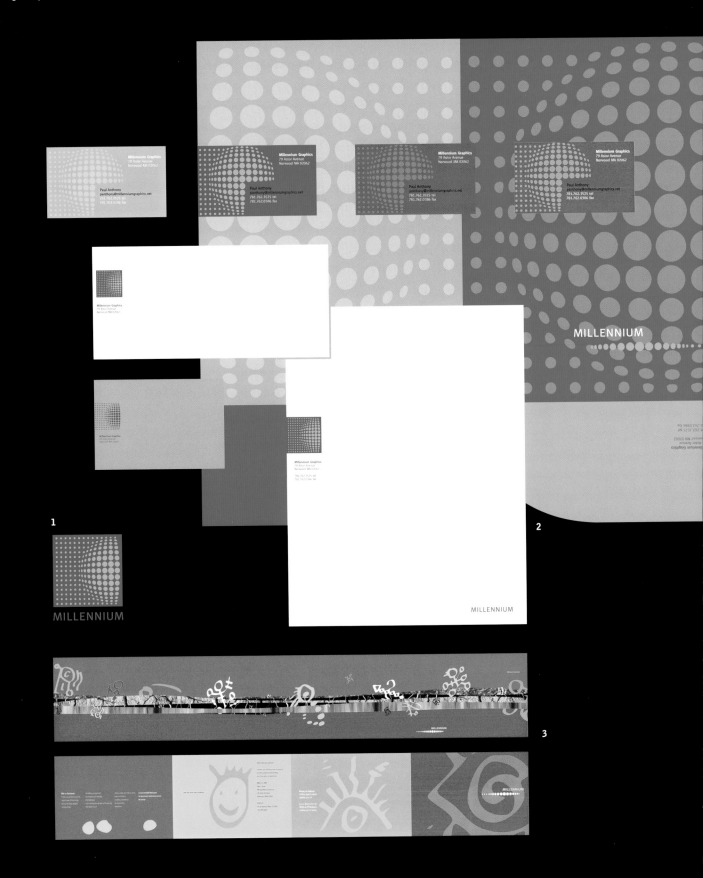

MILLENIUM GRAPHICS

1. Logo   **2.** Stationary System & Folder   **3.** Opening Celebration Invitation

Carleton

1

2

3

 PTC

Working
Relationships

4

5

6

 newmediary

7

8

9

LOGOS

1. Aura
Cards & Gifts

2. Carleton
Data Warehousing Technology

3. Lift
Private Personal Training Studio

4. Parametic Technology
Collaborative Product
Commerce Technology

5. Irislee
Custom Gift Programs

6. Working Relationships
Relationship Seminars & Counseling

7. Stone Center, Wellesley College
Psychological Research & Support
Center for Women & Families

8. Newmediary
Online RFP Marketplace

9. GiantSteps
Cooperative Gym Programs

ECOPY, INC.

1. Logo

2. Premium Support Brochure

3. Government Marketing Brochure

4. Corporate Brochure

5. Sales Tool: Binder & CD

6. Events Calendar

7. Product Overview &
Flash Sales Presentation

(top)

PRINCE LOBEL GLOVSKY & TYE LLP

1. Corporate Brochure　**2.** Web Site　**3.** Logo

(bottom)

WILSON ARCHITECTS

4. Logo　**5.** Corporate Brochure

(top)

EMERSON COLLEGE Undergraduate Admissions

1. Undergraduate Viewbook   **2.** Search Piece   **3.** Diversity (AHANA) Brochure

(bottom)

EMERSON COLLEGE Graduate Admissions

4. Graduate Viewbook   **5.** Direct Mail Postcard   **6.** Advertising Campaign

SOUTHBRIDGE

1. Southbridge Hotel, Conference Center,
Business Center, Various Signage

2. Visions Restaurant Logo

3. Focus Fitness Center Logo

4. Shades Restaurant & Bar Logo

Larsen Design + Interactive
7101 York Avenue South
Minneapolis, Minnesota 55435
888.590.4405

3500 Alameda de las Pulgas, Suite 100
Menlo Park, California 94025
888.590.4407

www.larsen.com
info@larsen.com

L A R S E N

At Larsen, it's the message that counts. The message expresses the brand and reaches the target audience. Understanding each client's strategic needs, Larsen creates visual and verbal messages that attract loyal customers and achieve business goals. That's why Larsen believes that communicating the right message to the right audience is simply good business.

The firm was founded in 1975 by Tim Larsen. As graphic designer, teacher, past president of the American Institute of Graphic Arts (AIGA) Minnesota, and AIGA national board member, he has attracted the best and brightest experienced leaders— in design, marketing, writing, interactive media, and account and project management. They are committed to excellence in design and service, creating an engaging culture. With a staff of 60 and expertise in many industries, Larsen can build the best creative team for each client.

Larsen's range of capabilities is broad— branding, identity, naming, print, packaging, interactive media, and environments. Across diverse media, Larsen ensures that the message remains clear. They combine creative sensibilities with strong business sense to deliver powerful results for companies large and small.

Take a look at the following pages. You'll see how Larsen takes complex information and brings fresh and inventive thought to each situation. The work has been designed under the leadership of creative vice presidents Jo Davison, Richelle Huff, Gayle Jorgens, David Shultz, Paul Wharton, and Nancy Whittlesey. Larsen has been nationally recognized by *Communication Arts, Graphis* and AIGA. But according to Tim Larsen, "Most importantly, our work creates successful results."

Larsen annual calendar featuring costumes designed for their 25th birthday gala.

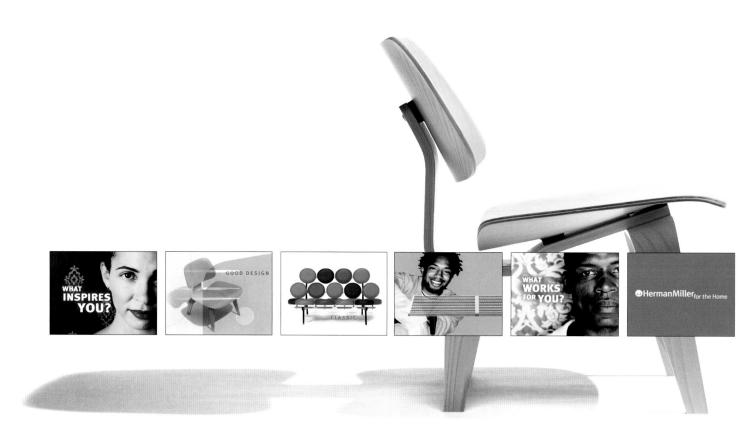

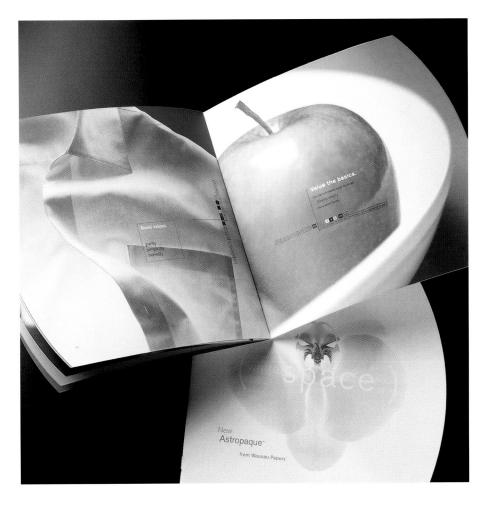

Herman Miller for the Home motion
graphics tradeshow video

Wausau Papers Astropaque
"White Space" paper promotion

Media Loft communications kit

Perfect Circle naming and wine
label design

Asyst Technologies Semicon West
tradeshow exhibit graphics

Target Stores iFix tools name,
identity, and packaging

American Express Partners Funds
launch materials

ING North American identity standards

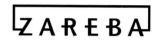

Boston Scientific identity

Target Corporation Grill It name and identity

Zareba name and identity

Nexen Group name and identity

UltraWheels identity

Children's Hospitals and Clinics identity

Appleton Coated Utopia Paper Web site

Novellus Systems annual report

Libera Design Inc.
Los Angeles, California 90064
San Francisco, California 94105
310.477.2027
www.liberadesign.com

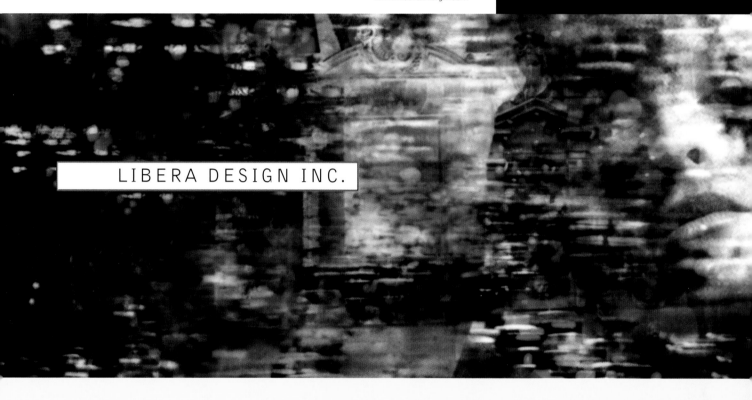

LIBERA DESIGN INC.

Leading design and marketing communications firm Libera Design Inc. offers a full spectrum of integrated, value-added design services to corporate clients. For more than 20 years, we have created designs that translate business positioning and strategies into functional visual communications.

As technology infiltrates the business environment, design is becoming increasingly standardized, losing impact and thus viewer interest. Whether a project is a corporate identity program, annual report, Web site, brochure or announcement, we find attention grabbing visual solutions that invite the audience to interact. Every job is approached as a creative opportunity.

We know corporate design is a service business. We recognize quality, value and responsiveness as driving factors in the fast-paced corporate world.

We believe that our experience, solution approach, business acumen and focus on service set us apart. And, our corporate clients, many at the forefront of their industries, agree.

At Libera Design, our ultimate goal is to partner with you to build a winning communication programs.

Libera Design Inc.

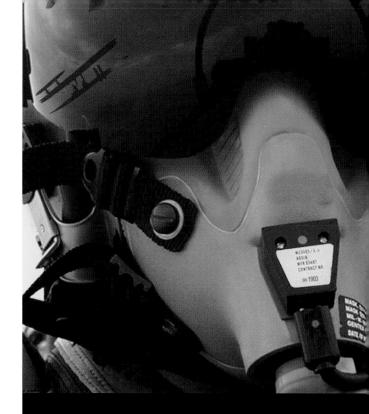

1.

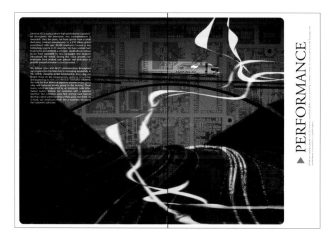

1. Fundamentals: value and opportunity for our customers, investors and employees – theme of Sanmina-SCI Annual Report

2. Adventure of Flight: 100 years – Marketing tool for the U.S. Navy Blue Angels

3. Power On, Repeat Performance, Play, Record, Store, Fast Forward: Zoran Annual Report and Marketing Tools

Change is inevitable. Good design assists clients take risks, exploring new territories, which can lead to fresh ideas.

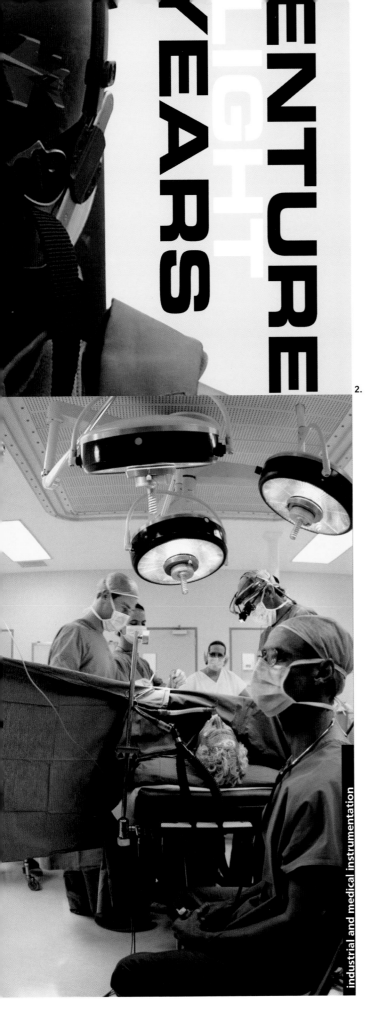

ENTURE LIGHT YEARS

industrial and medical instrumentation

2.

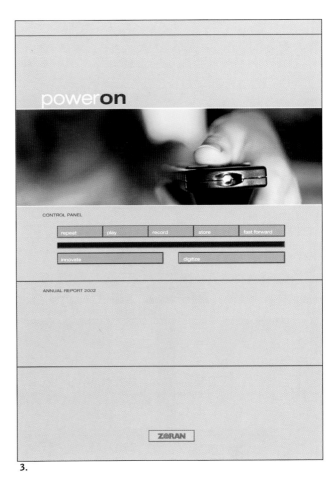

poweron

CONTROL PANEL

| repeat | play | record | store | fast forward |

| innovate | | digitize | |

ANNUAL REPORT 2002

ZORAN

3.

Power

TV VCR Cable DVD

1 2 3
4 5 6
7 8 9
+100 0 enter

Memory   TV/Video

Volume

Mute

Display   Surround   Caption   Aspect

Zoom   MTS/SAP   SAT/CABLE   VCR/DVD

ZORAN

Libera Design Inc.

CLIENT: SANMINA-SCI / SANM

GOALS / OBJECTIVES: For 10 years, we have partnered with Sanmina-SCI, a provider of premier contract manufacturing solutions, in creating a corporate identity. We began by designing the corporate logo, the most important visual branding tool, as well as a corporate look, reflecting the company's image. These visual images have been interwoven into Sanmina-SCI's communications materials – annual reports, marketing brochures, signage, etc. – to create an overall corporate image. More recently, we updated the image reflecting Sanmina's acquisition of SCI. Then we incorporated this new image into sales and marketing tools for use on both continents, meeting domestic and European size specifications.

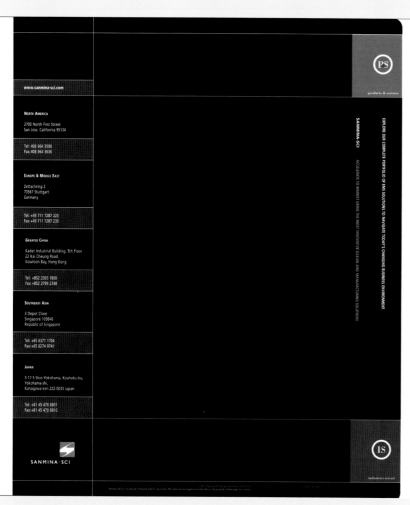

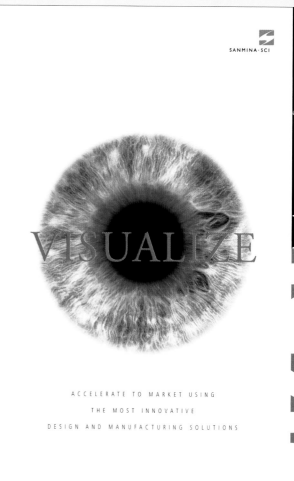

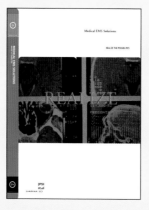

INDUSTRIES SERVED

SOLUTION / RESULTS: Teaming with Sanmina-SCI management, we worked to satisfy the key objective of designing sales and marketing materials that build business. Our solution – we designed a series of compelling, yet cost-effective tools that combined visual continuity with "reason why" text. First designed was the "Visualize the Opportunities," this was followed by a series of brochures entitled "Realize the Possibilities" and "Innovative to Drive Leadership" developed for different key audiences.

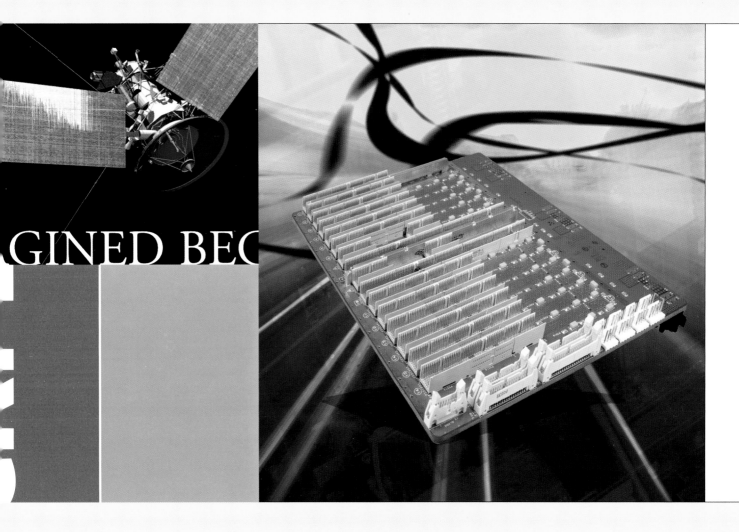

PRODUCTS & SERVICES

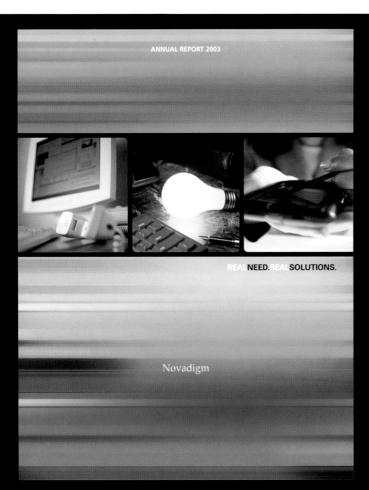

ANNUAL REPORT 2003

REAL NEED. REAL SOLUTIONS.

Novadigm

TO OUR SHAREHOLDERS

NOVADIGM'S SOLUTION: HANDLING SCALE, COMPLEXITY, AND RATE OF CHANGE

Royal & SunAlliance USA

WE SEE
OPPORTUNITIES
TO LEVERAGE...

INVESTORS like to make money.

investors
investors

We design annual reports that capture attention through creative visuals. We communica key messages through meaningful, hard-core images that tell a company's story and key investment messages to enhance shareholder value.

THINK OF THE POTENTIAL OF ENABLING
THOUSANDS UPON MILLIONS OF
INDIVIDUALS TO ACCESS WHAT HAS
PREVIOUSLY BEEN INACCESSIBLE.
...MAKE IT REAL.

9

connec

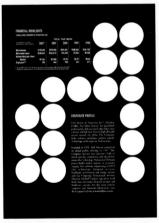

WE ARE EXPANDING
OUR HORIZONS...

EXPANDING OUR HORIZONS
2002 annual report

hall kinion

Libera Design Inc.

Image is Everything

Image communicates the intended message to a specific audience. With clients ranging from Borland, Litton Industries, Spelling Productions, AIG/SunAmerica – Kaufman and Broad, ARCO to UCLA Extension, we address a diverse audience.

Branding Shows Your Image

Branding reflects business strategy. Successful branding creates value, essential in the customer decision-making process to select one product or service over another. It creates an image in the customer's mind and ultimately leads to customer loyalty.

Our track record speaks for itself. We understand what it takes to communicate and create images that achieve results.

A Logo Tells the Story

1. Provider of contract Electronic Manufacturing Services – designed to communicate flexible, quick-turn and end-to-end manufacturing solutions.

2. Highly profitable publicly traded U.S. homebuilder – design intention was to simplify 5 elements down to 3 and retain memorability and equity in the name.

3. Innovative approach to blood cleaning – designed to show process of their system = before application, through their proprietary system and clean results.

4. Development through the partnership of company and city – designed to direct audience to this center.

5. Crowning of a top hotel property.

6. Manufacturer of herbal medications – designed to communicate use of multiple chemical fingerprints used in product development.

7. Venture capital firm – depicts success and upward momentum of this firm's global investment strategy

8. Holographic light display technology – depicts real-time, fourth dimension media for multiple applications

9. Recycling resources of Land, Air and Water.

10. Premier Century City property – designed prior to construction to assist with tenant leasing.

1.

Kaufman △ Broad

2.

CLEARANT, INC.

3.

KOLL ANAHEIM CENTER

4.

Hilton
International
Hotel

5.

PharmaPrint

6.

Intellect Capital Group, LLC

7.

QubicLight

8.

KAISER RESOURCES INC.

9.

1 9 9 9
AVENUE OF THE STARS

10.

168

LORENC YOO DESIGN

109 Vickery Street
Roswell, Georgia 30075
Tel.770.645.2828
jan@lorencyoodesign.com
www.lorencyoodesign.com

The Lorenc+Yoo Design (LYD) team boasts an impressive skill set including industrial design, architecture, furniture design, sculpture, and color theory. But, according to principal Jan Lorenc, the key to the firm's 25 years of success is a passion for crafting a good story. "We are storytellers and the narrative is the environment we create," says Lorenc. "The story is the client's mission."

This Roswell, Georgia-based firm identifies its work as "environmental communication design," a body of work which includes signage, retail spaces, furniture design, and exhibit design. This array of work is always carefully coordinated with a project team of architects, interior designers, landscape architects and others. The creative process remains the same regardless of the nature of the job - a holistic investigation into the client's organization to uncover their story. "Our approach looks at the company or environment and strives to incorporate the richness of its culture and context," says Lorenc.

Context for design is an important consideration in the LYD design process. The goal of each project is to create an integrated, seamless design approach that directly reflects the overall project intent. This approach results in projects with true design significance and longevity. LYD gains knowledge of an overall project, the goal of the team, and conceives a project that responds to historical or temporal context. In the end it is the story, the client's story, which organizes the message and engages the public.

1.

2.

3.

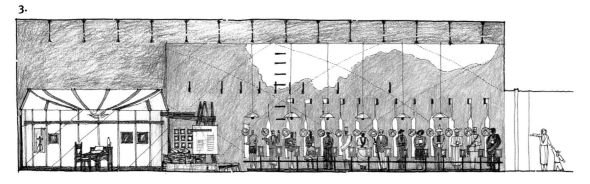

Wordspring Discovery Center

1. Overhead view of visitors center

2. Figure wall

3. Sketch of figure wall and well

4. Translation area

5. Language tree

6. Sketch of language tree

4.

5.

6.

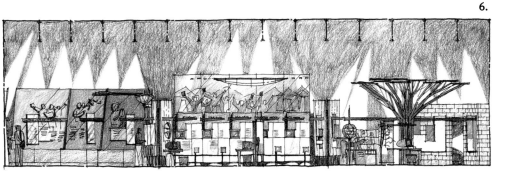

2.

1.

Sony Ericsson

1. Product Stage and upper conference room

2. Computer model of exhibit

3. Front view of 'S' and 'E'

4. Sketch of product stage

5. Floor plan of lower level

6. Product displays

7. Floor plan of upper level

8. Sketch of conference room

9. Upper level conference room

3.

4.

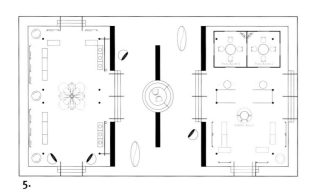

5.

6.

9.

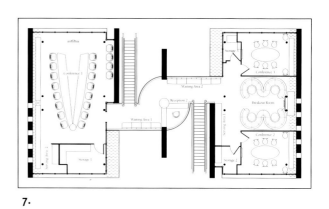

7.

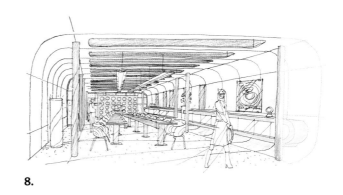

8.

1.

2.

Haworth, Inc.

1. Entrance and reception area

2. Sketch of entrance

3. Detail of video globe

4. Product universe

5. Sketch of brand messaging

6. Customer stories

7. Chair wall product display

3.

4.

5.

6.

7.

1.

McWane Newsroom

1. Interior view

2. Light sequence on the entrance sign

3. Main entrance with sign and sculpture

2.

3.

325 W. Huron, Suite 812
Chicago, IL 60610

MLR DESIGN

MLR Design, formerly known as Murrie Lienhart
Rysner & Associates, is a brand identity design
firm with a 36-year history, which includes
working with some of the world's most
successful brands and companies. Comprised of
strategists, designers and production specialists,
we work together to deliver programs for new
brands, brand revitalization and brand restaging.
Our promise is to meet the objectives of every
assignment with strategically focused design that
is on time and on budget. We invite you to
discover who we are and how our team might
assist you in your brand-building efforts.

1

2

3

4

6

7

8

Alka-
Seltzer®
ANTACID & PAIN RELIEVER

9

10

Cottonelle

11

5

1. Wild Cherry Pepsi packaging restage in collaboration with the Pepsi Design Group.

2. Jobe's Fertilizer Spikes packaging restage for Easy Gardener, Inc.

3. Creme Savers new brand packaging for Kraft Confections.

4. Skippy packaging revitalization for Unilever Best Foods.

5. SKYY Blue new brand packaging for Miller Brewing Company.

6. Carter's brand logo and packaging restage for The William Carter Company.

7. Bounce new brand logo for The Procter & Gamble Company.

8. Seven Seas brand logo revitalization for Kraft Foods, Inc.

9. Alka Seltzer brand logo revitalization for Bayer Corporation.

10. Toll House brand logo revitalization for Nestle USA, Inc.

11. Cottonelle brand logo revitalization for Kimberly-Clark Inc.

1

2

3

4

1. Carefree Koolerz new brand packaging for Kraft Confections.

2. Cetaphil packaging revitalization for Galderma Laboratories, L.P.

3. Gatorade Energy Drink new brand packaging for The Quaker Oats Company.

4. Splash 'n Go new brand packaging for Kimberly-Clark, Inc.

5. Kinley packaging revitalization for The Coca-Cola Company.

6. Satori new brand packaging and naming for Kaytee Products, Inc.

5   6

6

8

7

9

2

3

1

4

1. Chicago Cutlery packaging restage for World Kitchen, Inc.

2. Gatorade Ice new sub-brand packaging for The Quaker Oats Company.

3. Simply Orange new brand packaging for The Minute Maid Company.

4. Bugs Bunny vitamin packaging revitalization for Bayer Corporation.

5. Dasani new brand packaging for The Coca-Cola Company.

6. Quaker Chewy brand logo and packaging revitalization for The Quaker Oats Company.

7. Keebler brand logo restage for Keebler Foods Company.

8. H20 Plus new brand logo, signage and packaging for H20 Plus.

9. Banana Boat brand logo and packaging revitalization for Playtex Products, Inc.

5

Weiman packaging restage for
The Herbert Stanley Company, LLC.

Selbert Perkins Design
200 Culver Blvd.
Playa del Rey, California 90293
tel: 310.822.5223 fax: 310.822.5203
mkruchko@spdwest.com

11 Water Street
Arlington, Massachusetts 02476
tel: 781.574.6605 fax: 781.574.6606
ereed@spdeast.com

SELBERT PERKINS DESIGN COLLABORATIVE

Selbert Perkins Design is strategic brand development and design firm with offices in California and Massachusetts.

SPD is committed to providing clients with the strategies and expertise needed in a variety of disciplines—branding, print, environmental and interactive.

Selbert Perkins range of brand development and design services includes:
- Advertising
- Annual Reports
- Brand Strategy & Research
- Branded Environments
- City/Streetscapes
- Corporate Branding
- Identity Development
- Interactive Media
- Naming Systems
- Product & Package Design
- Print Media
- Public Art & Sculpture
- Signage & Wayfinding

The work of Selbert Perkins Design can be seen throughout a broad range of clients, across the United States and Asia.
- Agile Gardens, Guangzhou, China
- Bingham McCutchen, Boston, MA
- Canal City Hakata, Fukuoka, Japan
- Catholic Healthcare West, Los Angeles, CA
- Downtown Disney, Anaheim, CA
- Highmark Funds, Los Angeles, CA
- Jewish Children's Museum, NYC, NY
- Los Angeles International Airport, CA
- Marina del Rey, CA
- Miami Children's Museum, Miami, FL
- Millenia Walk, Singapore
- MotorCities, Detroit, MI
- New York Botanical Garden, NYC, NY
- Pacific Design Center, Los Angeles, CA
- Universal Studios, Los Angeles, CA and Orlando, FL
- University of Southern California, Los Angeles, CA

The guiding principle behind the work of Selbert Perkins Design is to create design solutions that inform, educate, and entertain people around the world through the power of art, communications and environments.

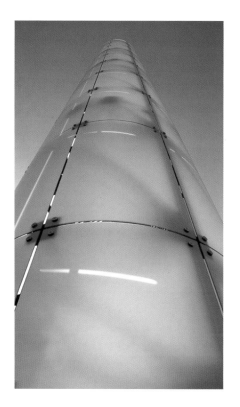

LAX
Los Angeles World Airports

1.

EPTDESIGN

1. Los Angeles World Airports, Los Angeles, CA—naming system, identity development, branded environment, monumental gateway, signs and wayfinding.

2. EPT Design, Pasadena, CA— brand strategy, identity development, print media and interactive media.

2.

HIGHMARK
FUNDS

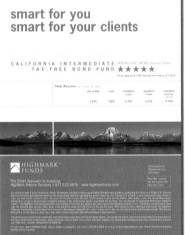

1.

1. Highmark Funds, Los Angeles, CA—brand strategy, architecture and research, annual reports, print media.

2. Vina Walk, Ebina, Japan— branded environment and signage and wayfinding system for a mixed use development.

2.

BINGHAM McCUTCHEN

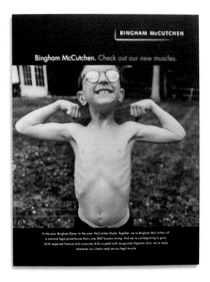

Bingham McCutchen, Boston, MA—brand strategy, architecture and research, annual reports, print media, advertising, interactive media, and branded environment.

MotorCities, Automobile National Heritage Area,
Detroit, MI—brand identity development, print
media, interactive media and branded
environment.

Pacific Design Center, Los Angeles, CA—main entrance identity signs and monumental sculptural elements.

SHIMOKOCHI-REEVES
113 N. San Vicente Blvd. Suite 300
Beverly Hills, CA 90211-2326
P: 323.655.0550
F: 323.655.0850
E: info@shimokochi-reeves.com
www.shimokochi-reeves.com

SHIMOKOCHI-REEVES

Unparalleled Experience United Airlines, United Way, and California Cheese, are among the well known identities created by designer Mamoru Shimokochi. Both he and partner Anne Reeves boast roots with Saul Bass & Associates, the internationally acclaimed pioneer of brand identity and package design. Coupled with Mamoru's 30-year track record in brand design excellence, Anne brings 25 years' design and marketing expertise to the partnership. Together, Shimokochi-Reeves enjoys the perfect blend of Mamoru's creative passion and Anne's market-driven sense of purpose.

Personal Responsiveness Unencumbered by the many layers of larger firms, Shimokochi-Reeves nurtures a highly personal, responsive relationship with their clients. Partners Anne and Mamoru gain a thorough understanding of each client's marketing goals by working face to face as a strategic partner. The result is creative strategies that go the extra mile to yield true competitive edge.

Powerful Branding Solutions Brands have just seconds to connect with their target audience. Shimokochi-Reeves delivers fresh, engaging designs that foster instant recall, speaking to the hearts and minds of consumers. As the brand design expert, Shimokochi-Reeves creates powerful, market-driven solutions that achieve results!

Natural High brand identity and package revitalization
Gourmet entrées and desserts for backpackers
Richmoor Corporation

Silk Soymilk packaging
Brand extension to a new Silk single-serve line
White Wave, Inc.

BONK brand name, brand identity and packaging system
New hair styling brand targeting Gen Y
Wella Corporation

Color Preserve brand identity and packaging system
New brand for the professional hair salon
Wella Corporation

SOOHOO DESIGNERS

1424 Marcelina Avenue
Torrance, CA 90501
Phone: 310.381.0170
Fax: 310.381.0169
www.soohoodesign.com

1

2

1. Fund-raising campaign brochure and invitation for the Asian American Symphony.
2. Professional product line brochure for Epson America, Inc.
3. Capabilities brochure for GSC, a management consulting firm.

GSC works with you to accomplish both your short and long-term goals. We offer practical and executable solutions as we help you prepare your people and develop highly effective, integrated teams.

Our approach creates self-sufficiency because we believe that the best results occur when you manage without being dependent on us.

Our mission, simply, is to guide you in articulating a clear vision of a more compelling and promising future and showing you how to realize it.

4

5

6

7

8

9

10

11

12

11. Printer promotion for Epson America, Inc.
12. Information kit for Blue Cross of California.
13. Promotional stationery for Elar Partners.
14. Tangram puzzle self-promotion for
    SooHoo Designers.

13

14

We solve marketing communication needs
in a collaborative environment utilizing
sound strategies, inspired creative and
strong partnerships. Our solutions speak
to a deep emotional core, touching people
in ways that affect their feelings, their
perceptions and the choices they make.

Sunspots Creative
51 Newark Street
Suite 204
Hoboken, NJ 07030
201.459.9199
info@sunspotscreative.com
www.sunspotscreative.com

SUNSPOTS CREATIVE

Clean. Bold. Energetic. These are the words that best describe the design emanating from Sunspots Creative, one of the country's most highly acclaimed young studios for innovation and creativity.

Located in the scenic waterfront city of Hoboken, Sunspots Creative considers itself a hybrid agency offering a complete range of advertising, design and multimedia services.

"Our clients like our versatility because we can design all of their collateral materials and, in turn, not miss a beat when it comes to developing their advertising as well," says Sunspots principal Rick Bonelli. Together with his business partner, Deena Hartley, this tandem has built its reputation by developing a variety of unique, three-dimensional, handmade sales promotions, bold identity graphics and breakthrough advertising campaigns.

Sunspots Creative is known for work that stands out from the ordinary. However,

most important, the studio's proprietary designs still correctly situate its clients in the most favorable position within their respective marketplaces. Sunspots believes that every client possesses an individual aspect and personality of their business that sets them apart in their field. The key is to uncover this individual trait, perfect it through striking graphics and powerful messages and reinforce the brand in every conceivable application.

Another strength that has fostered the growth of Sunspots Creative is the excellent rapport and respect it holds for its clientele. "It all comes down to a matter of trust and understanding between both parties," emphasizes Rick. "We listen to and value the input and direction of our clients, but ultimately, want to take their expectations beyond the boundaries of what they may have been envisioning."

Originality. Collaboration. Trust. That's what great design is all about.

Identity Crisis
a self-promotional 3-D branding booklet

Mom lied.

Call us to dispell any myths and concerns regarding the methods, benefits and costs of the revolutionary Excimer Laser Refractive Surgery (PRK and LASIK) procedure.

REFRACTIVE SURGERY CENTERS OF NEW JERSEY
CLIFTON, NJ 973.473.1515 • CHESTER, NJ 908.879.7297

Temporary solution.

Call us to discuss a permanent solution to needing glasses or contacts with the revolutionary Excimer Laser Refractive Surgery (PRK and LASIK) procedure.

REFRACTIVE SURGERY CENTERS OF NEW JERSEY
CLIFTON, NJ 973.473.1515 • CHESTER, NJ 908.879.7297

1

NEW JERSEY SCHOOL OF ACUPUNCTURE

3

the English Channel

4

1. Ads for laser vision correction for Refractive Surgery Centers of New Jersey
2. Brochure for Corporate Jet Support
3. New Jersey School of Acupuncture logo
4. Logo for The English Channel, a trading company for British music memorabilia
5. Gulf Tags trade show promotion for Corporate Jet Support
6. 3-D promotional holiday mailers for Accudart
7. Image brochure for The Digital Loop
8. Classic Athletic Club newspaper ad
9. Transit ads for Innovative Sports Marketing

2

5

6

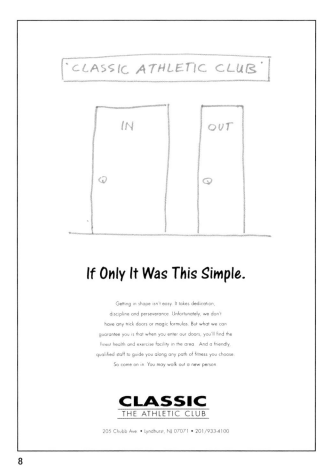

8

If Only It Was This Simple.

Getting in shape isn't easy. It takes dedication, discipline and perseverance. Unfortunately, we don't have any trick doors or magic formulas. But what we can guarantee you is that when you enter our doors, you'll find the finest health and exercise facility in the area. And a friendly, qualified staff to guide you along any path of fitness you choose. So come on in. You may walk out a new person.

CLASSIC
THE ATHLETIC CLUB

205 Chubb Ave. • Lyndhurst, NJ 07071 • 201/933-4100

9

7

1

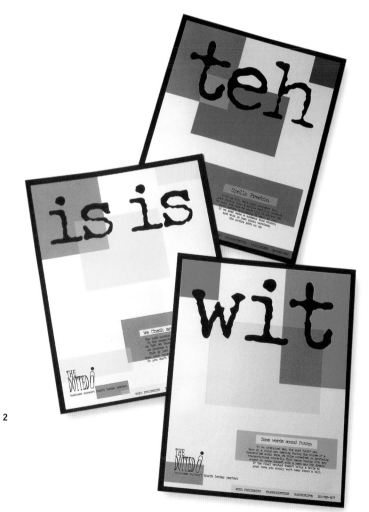

2

3

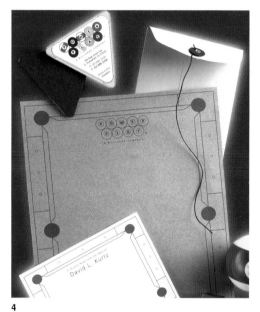

4

5

1. 3-D press release for dealers for Studio Tac, dry adhesive transfer sheets from Letraset

2. Trade ads for The Dotted i, a business support service

3. CD packaging for Lucent Technologies

4. Identity system for Power Play, a billiards company

5. Direct mail piece for The Digital Loop, a prepress and digital asset management company

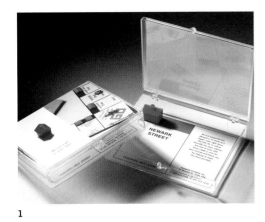

1

2

3

4

5

6

7

8

1. 3-D moving announcement for Sunspots Creative

2. Soldier in a Box, a pro bono gift item for local VFW chapters to promote patriotism following 9-11-01

3. Self-promotional logo deck for Sunspots Creative

4. Media kit for GSS Security Systems

5. Packaging for Synergy Originals, an aromatherapy line

6. Promotional direct mailer for Alphamat Artcare matboard for photographers from NielsenBainbridge

7. Logo for a sales incentive program for NielsenBainbridge

8. Logo for Silverstein Ophthalmology Group

1

4

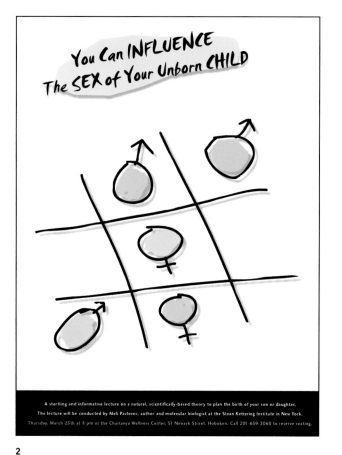

2

5

3

1. Trade ad for Accudart announcing the merger of two companies
(one in London, the other in New York)

2. Poster for the Chaitanya Wellness Center for a lecture on child planning

3. Logo for Etrana, an internet group buying and e-transaction company

4. Identity system for The Dotted i

5. Call for Entries posters for The New Jersey Advertising Club

1

2

3

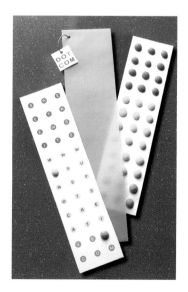

4

5

215

1

2

3

4

5

1. Jar Yer Memory, a Sunspots promotional holiday gift

2. Digital craftsman brochure for Premium Color Graphics

3. Identity system for Soleil Bronze, a tanning salon

4. Identity system for Alpine Printing

5. Identity system for Sunspots Creative

Sunspots

1730 M Street NW, Suite 600
Washington, DC 20036
202.835.1100
www.supon.com

SUPON DESIGN GROUP

Founded in 1988 in the nation's capital, Supon Design Group has established itself as one of America's leading studios. In 15 years, the firm has grown from a one-person, minority-owned graphics studio into an international enterprise specializing in identity, collateral, and new media design. In 1999, the studio merged with the full-service agency, MHI. Supon Design Group's top-notch design skills are now complemented by advertising, marketing, event and video production services, all located in our downtown D.C. headquarters.

At Supon Design Group, our clientele is varied: Early on founder Supon Phornirunlit and his team made a conscious decision not to specialize in any one industry or type of project. Instead, we work with a wide range of organizations in the non-profit, government, commercial, and educational sectors — both in the U.S. and abroad. Because of the diversity of audiences, our creative remains fresh and our approach, focused.

Over 1,000 awards, including recognition from most every creative organization, competition, and publication, testify not only to our superior creativity, but to our strategic thinking and appropriateness of solution. Supon Design Group has been profiled in various national and international publications, including *HOW, Art4D, Page, Novum, Studio* and *Asia Inc.* Our work has been featured in creative media, including *Step-by-Step, Graphis, Print,* and *Communications Arts.* Further recognition has included Best-in-Show ADDY wins in both print and new media — the latter for our own website, www.supon.com.

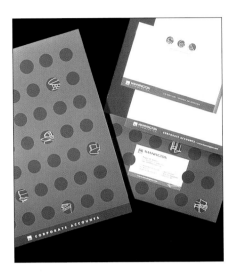
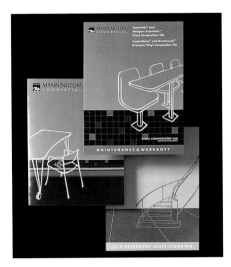

Mannington Commercial, Sales material identity
for flooring manufacturer

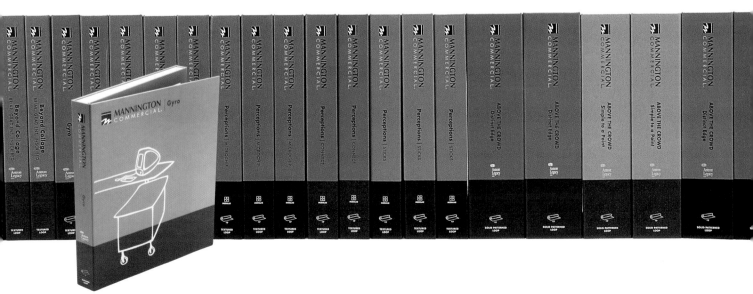

Lehman-Smith + McLeish, Website for architectural firm

1

2

3

4

5

6

7

8

1. Cow Parade, Logo

2. World Amateur Team Championships –
   Puerto Rico, Golf event logo

3. Washington Metropolitan Area Transit
   Authority, Arts program logo

4. CoquiCo, Toy company logo

5. Advertising Club of Metropolitan Washington,
   Awards identity

6. Newspaper Association of America,
   Conference identity

7. Hanger Orthopedic Group, Annual report

8. Washington Humane Society, Annual report

CoquiCo, Tourism marketing identity, including posters and products

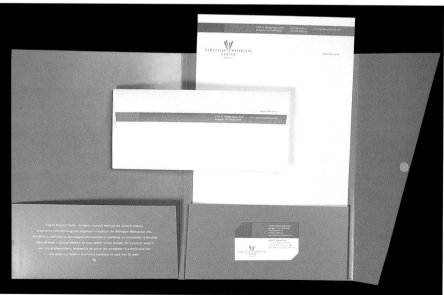

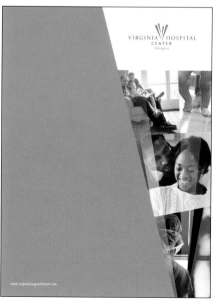

Virginia Hospital Center, Brand identities for institution and specializations

1

2

3

4

5

savantage solutions

6

ONPOINT
DIGITAL

7

8

ESSD
AFRICA

9

1. Chesapeake Wine Company

2. Beanstalk Group

3. Litigation Communications

4. Hill and Knowlton for Johnson & Johnson
   Caregivers Program

5. Z-Bears, Toy company

6. Savantage Solutions

7. OnPoint Digital

8. AdviceZone.com

9. World Bank Environmentally and Socially
   Sustainable Development Network program

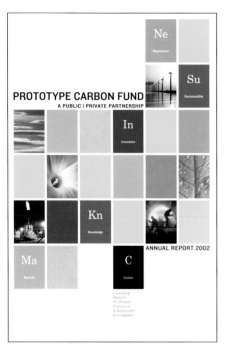

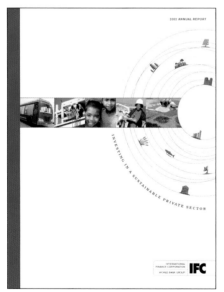

1. World Bank Prototype Carbon Fund,
   Annual report

2. International Finance Corporation,
   Annual report

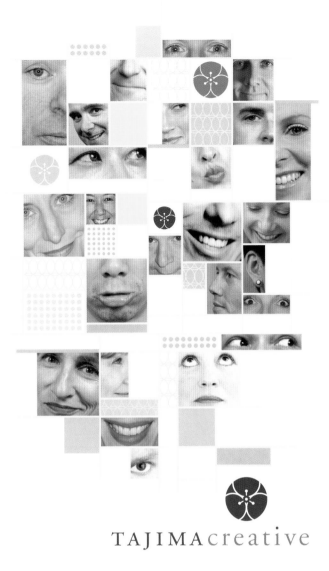

Tajima Creative
1700 El Camino Real
Menlo Park, California 94025
ph 650.325.9316
fx 650.323.6930
tajimacreative.com

TAJIMAcreative

Established in 1996 by Elaine Tajima, Tajima Creative is a visual communications and marketing services group that uses a more flexible, non-traditional business model to meet client needs. Tajima Creative believes the best creative work often happens outside the office, which is why its award-winning design professionals are located all over the country. The "hub and spoke" approach begins with a strategic group of experienced strategists, client leads, and art directors stationed in the Menlo Park "hub." The creative "spokes" of the team – its cutting-edge artists, trend experts, illustrators, designers, and writers – are sprinkled throughout the U.S.

Tajima Creative believes in getting to know a client's business inside and out. In fact, that's what has made the group flourish in the most challenging of economies. The strategists view themselves as extensions of the corporate clients they serve.

"Offering great creative isn't enough," says Elaine Tajima. "We go the extra mile for our clients, forming relationships built on service, reliability and trust. In today's world, meaningful relationships are everything."

1

2

nSite Software, Inc.

3

1. Turner/Martin
   Website and Product Catalog

2. WM Group of Funds
   Identity and Collateral System

3. nSITE Software
   Identity and Business System

4. Orange County
   Tradeshow Exhibit

4

1

2

3

1. Washington Mutual
   NY Market Entry Merchandising Campaign
   and Display Windows

2. Tax Homme
   Identity, Business System and Website

3. Center Trust
   Annual Report and Collateral

4. Cedarbrook
   Identity, Collateral and Exhibits

4

A New Chapter in Children's Books is Here!

The First Page

Fine Children's Books

Award Winning Literature
Storytime Everyday
Books for Kids age 0 - 14

The First Page 270 E. 17th Street (at Santa Ana Ave.) in Costa Mesa
Next to "Where's The Party"
949.645.KIDS

1

2

3

1. First Page
   Identity, Print Ad and Store Design

2. Washington Mutual
   School Savings Program Collateral and Premiums

3. Washington Mutual Home Loans
   Realtor/Broker Direct Mail Premium

4. Washington Mutual
   "A Pig For All Reasons" Trend Shop and Product

4

1

2

1. Adhesive Software
   Tradeshow Collateral and Booth Graphics
2. Naartjie
   Holiday Windows and Graphic Package

Tom Graboski Associates, Inc. Design
4649 Ponce de Leon Blvd.
Suite 401
Coral Gables, Florida 33146
305.669.2550
mail@tgadesign.com
www.tgadesign.com

TOM GRABOSKI ASSOCIATES, INC. DESIGN

Founded in 1980, Tom Graboski Associates,
Inc., Design is an internationally recognized
multidisciplinary Graphic Design firm
located in Coral Gables, Florida. Our
diversity of talent and experience enable us
to provide consistently innovative and
effective graphic solutions for corporate
brand identity, environmental graphic
design, wayfinding, exhibit and themed
design as well as industrial/interior
design projects.

Environmental Graphic Design is our
specialty, but our knowledge and skill in a
variety of design disciplines allows us to
provide expert solutions to any challenge.
Our versatility affords us the ability to
provide a "total package" - from a new
identity to a new environment.. We
welcome the exciting opportunities and
possibilities that new and emerging
technologies affords our clients—as
well as the growth and evolution of our
design studio.

Biltmore Hotel Identity and Wayfinding Signage **1,2**

Marriot Harbor Beach Resort Restaurant Identity **3**

Ritz Carlton Key Biscayne Identity and Wayfinding Signage **4,5**

Espirito Santo Plaza Identity and Wayfinding Signage **6**

6

1

2

3

4

5

1

2

3

4

5

Parrot Jungle Island Identity and Wayfinding Signage **1,2,3,4**

Fairchild Tropical Gardens Identity and Wayfinding Signage **5,6,7**

6

7

2

1

3

4

Health Central Hospital Identity and Wayfinding Signage **1,2,3**

Homestead Hospital Identity and Wayfinding Signage **4**

University of Miami Jackson Hospital
Identity and Wayfinding Signage **1,2,3**

South Miami Hospital
Identity and Wayfinding Signage **4,5,6**

4

5

6

1

2

3

1

2

DADELAND
CENTRE 4

3

Streets of Mayfair Identity and Wayfinding Signage **1,2,3**

Logo for Office Building **4**

Logo for Hotel Spa **5**

THE SPA
MARRIOTT'S
HARBOR
BEACH 5

3

CURTIS + ROGERS

The Collection Showroom Graphics **1,2**

Logo for Landscape Architecture firm **3**

1

2

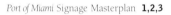

1

2

3

Port of Miami Signage Masterplan **1,2,3**

Universal Studios Islands of Adventure Identity and Wayfinding Signage **4,5,6**

4

5

6

Anabela Alves

 Simon Benjamin

 John Bruno

 Stan Church

 Wendy Church

 Tangerine Clarke

 Jeremy Creighton

 Allen Gaoiran

 Lawrence Haggerty

 Jhomy Irrazaba

 Stacey Kelley

 Camilla Kristiansen

 Dustin Longstreth

 Venise Maybank

 Clare Reece-Raybould

 Richard Rickaby

 Jessica Shafran

 Amy Shaw

 Lucian Toma

 Rob Wallace

 Susan Wiley

 Janet Willemain

Akira Yasuda

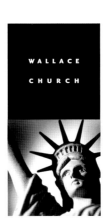

Wallace Church, Inc.
Strategic Brand Identity
330 East 48th Street
New York, NY 10017
212-755-2903
info@wallacechurch.com
www.wallacechurch.com

WALLACE CHURCH, INC.

Making a brand out-perform the competition is our primary goal. Simply put, we measure our success by our brands' successes. With our proprietary Visual Exploratory Process™, a proven method of strategic inquiry, we provide a precise analytical tool for marketers and designers. Sophisticated and reality-based, VEP helps define central issues, targets customer motivations and eliminates information clutter.

At Wallace Church, every project is tailored to fit specific objectives. "Sharing our clients' business concerns is critical to us," says founding partner Stan Church. "The uncompromised commitment of our highly talented creative and marketing staff is the decisive success factor."

With more than 25 years of experience in packaging and structural design, brand name develoment, brand identity creation and retail environment design, Wallace Church is an industry leader – one of the top full-service brand imagery and package design resources in the country. We are fortunate to be the recipient of hundreds of awards, both nationally and internationally. With worldwide affiliates in top markets, major clients in virtually every consumer product category and an international design team, Wallace Church has the insight and the expertise to build long-term brand loyalty and to turn challenges into growth opportunities.

2

3

4

1 Red Stripe Beer Bottle Caps
2 Pollio Italian Cheese
3 ZYGO Energy Vodka
4 Ciao Bella Gelatos and Sorbettos
5 Oasis Nutritional Bar
6 Zazz Beverage Design

5

6

2

3

4

1 Wallace Church 2001 New Year "Robot Clock"
2 Wallace Church Thanksgiving "Wishbone"
3 Wallace Church Baseball Invite
4 Wallace Church Corporate Identity Icons
5 Wallace Church Fall Wine "Turning of the Leaves"
6 Wallace Church Corporate Identity

5

6

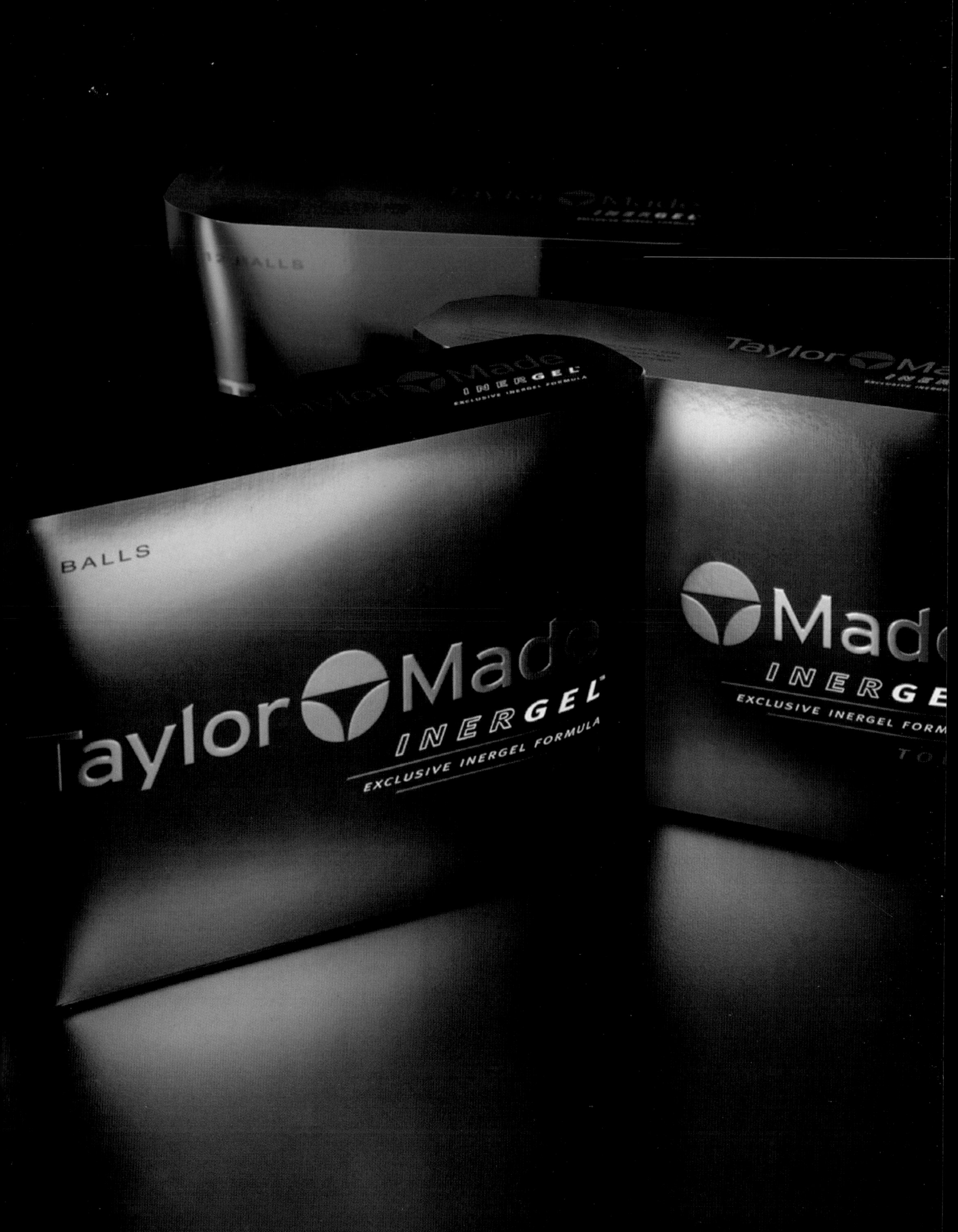
BALLS
INERGEL
EXCLUSIVE INERGEL FORMULA

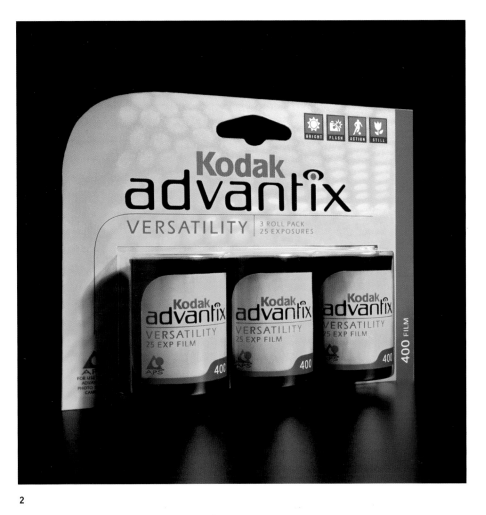

2

3

4

5

6

7

1 Taylor Made Inergel Packaging System
2 Kodak Advantix Package
3 Kodak Icons
4 Kodak Black and White Film Concept
5 Taylor Made Inergel Illustration
6 American Beauty Packaging Concept
7 Main Street Beverage Design

1

2

1 Relax, Renew, Revive Packaging
2 Relax, Renew, Revive Fragrance Illustrations
3 Gillette Mach3 Turbo Packaging

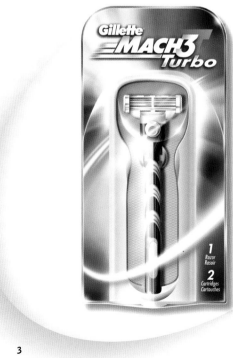

3